Sawai Man Singh II
of Jaipur

LIFE AND LEGEND

R.P. SINGH
KANWAR RAJPAL SINGH

FOREWORD BY
SAWAI BHAWANI SINGH

LOTUS COLLECTION
ROLI BOOKS

Lotus Collection

This edition first published in 2005
The Lotus Collection
An imprint of
Roli Books Pvt. Ltd.
M-75, G.K. II Market
New Delhi 110 048
Phones: ++91 (11) 2921 2271, 2921 2782
2921 0886, Fax: ++91 (11) 2921 7185
E-mail: roli@vsnl.com; Website: rolibooks.com
Also at
Varanasi, Bangalore, Jaipur

Editor : Dipa Chaudhuri
Cover Design : Arati Subramanyam
Layout Design : Narendra Shahi

ISBN: 81-7436-400-5

Typeset in Fairfield LH Light by Roli Books Pvt. Ltd. and

MAN SINGH ASSUMED RULING POWERS AS THE
39TH RULER OF JAIPUR ON 14 MARCH 1931, ON
THE STRENGTH OF ARTICLE8 OF THE TREATY OF
1818 BETWEEN THE EAST INDIA COMPANY AND
HIS HIGHNESS MAHARAJA SAWAI JAGAT SINGH,
THE 35TH RULER OF JAIPUR, WHICH READS
AS UNDER:

THE MAHARAJA AND HIS HEIRS AND
SUCCESSORS SHALL REMAIN ABSOLUTE RULERS
OF THEIR TERRITORY AND THEIR DEPENDENTS
ACCORDING TO LONG ESTABLISHED USAGE.

CONTENTS

ACKNOWLEDGEMENTS

We owe profound gratitude to HH Rajmata Gayatri Devi of Jaipur for all the hours she spared to talk about the late HH Sawai Man Singh II. Special thanks are also due to HH Brigadier Sawai Bhawani Singh, MVC, of Jaipur for kindly writing the Foreword for this book, HH Padmani Devi of Jaipur, Princess Diya Kumari and Maharaja Narendra Singh, for providing invaluable information and allowing us access to all papers at City Palace, as well as to the HH Sawai Man Singh II Museum Trust.

Profound thanks are due to HH Gaj Singh of Jodhpur for sparing his valuable time to provide interesting insights into those times.

Thanks are also due to Chand Baisa, the late HH's favourite sister, Gopal Narayan Bahura, Major Sumer Singh Naila, Thakur Mohan Singh Kanota, Pratap Singh Pachkodia, Thakurani Sneh Govind Singh, Laxman Singh Barwara, Yogendra Sahai, Suraj Kumawat, and Shailendra Kr. Singhal.

Finally, we must thank Cheryl D' Souza, Rashmi Sharma and Florence Santos for their help in preparing the manuscript, and their advice and judgment in the selection of the material.

The City Palace

Jaipur

FOREWORD

B orn on 21 August 1911, Kanwar Mor Mukut Singh was the second son of Thakur Sawai Singh of Isarda. Chosen for adoption by Maharaja Sawai Madho Singh II on 24 March 1921, he was named Sawai Man Singh II.

Sawai Man Singh II was the right choice as heir to the throne of Jaipur, as he showed great promise from the time of adoption, and later proved worthy of the throne to the fullest as an able ruler, statesman, and administrator, to become a legend in his lifetime. The death of his adoptive father, the then ruler of Jaipur, Maharaja Sawai Madho Singh II in 1922, however, left him vulnerable to challenges at the tender age of eleven.

Since Sawai Man Singh II was a minor at the time of accession, the period from 1922 to 1931 was administered by a European President under the Regency Council.

He received his initial education at Mayo College, Ajmer, and after a short stint was sent abroad for further studies. He received his military training at the Royal Military Academy, Woolwich, England. He was the first and the last Indian prince to serve in the King's Life Guards—this will remain a permanent and indeed a rare distinction. After his return to

Jaipur in October 1930, he was invested with the full ruling powers of a maharaja in March 1931.

The many reforms and developments in almost all fields achieved during the period of Maharaja Sawai Ram Singh II gained momentum during my father's time, and several prominent educational centres, administrative buildings, the Sanganer Airport, and more, were established in his time.

My father rendered valuable service in World War II, and actively visited the warfronts as a Liaison Officer of the Indian State Force. Needless to say, his visits to the front were an immense morale booster for the forces. The Jaipur State Force, that is, the Sawai Man Guards—the unit that was raised and trained by my father himself—rendered commendable service in World War II. The other Jaipur State Forces which also rendered commendable service were the Kachhwaha Horse, First and Second Battalions, and the Transport Corps.

My father held the rank of Captain in the British Army, and that of Lieutenant General in the Indian Army. He invested the positions he held with dignity and distinction, and performed his duties with earnestness and devotion. He was a tough taskmaster and a strict disciplinarian when it came to discharging duties and responsibilities. He was known for his unfailing punctuality, his eye for detail, his immaculate habits and impeccable nature.

Immediately after his accession, my father got very deeply involved in the development of Jaipur, and the uplift of the people.

1947 and 1949 were eventful years in his life. In 1947, the Silver Jubilee of his accession to the throne was celebrated with great pomp and show. On 30 March 1949, he took oath as the Rajpramukh of Rajasthan in the presence of Sardar Vallabhbhai Patel.

In 1962, he was elected as a member of the Rajya Sabha and also appointed Ambassador to Spain.

An internationally renowned polo player, he led the Jaipur

Polo Team from victory to victory, and established a record by winning all the tournaments in which his team played. In 1957, his team topped up the Victory Crown by winning the World Gold Cup Championship in Deauville, France.

Destiny, however, would soon take a ruthless turn. On 24 June 1970, he died after a fall from his pony during a game of polo in Cirencester Park in England. The news of his sudden and tragic death came as a rude shock to all of us, to the world, leaving us stunned with a sense of an irreparable loss.

In the field of sports, not only was he an internationally acclaimed polo player, but he was also outstanding in hockey, cricket, football and tennis. At Mayo College, he won the Viceroy's Medal, awarded to the most outstanding sportsman.

He married thrice: the first marriage, in 1924, was with Marudhar Kanwar, the daughter of Maharaja Sardar Singh of Jodhpur; the second marriage, in 1932, was with Kishore Kanwar, the daughter of Maharaja Sumer Singh, also of Jodhpur. The two Maharanis were related to each other as aunt and niece. The third marriage, in 1940, was with Shrimati Gayatri Devi, daughter of the Late Maharaja Bahadur of Cooch Behar. She is presently the Rajmata Saheba of Jaipur.

My father was a dignified prince with a charming personality, and was loved and revered by all his people.

Jaipur and its people were his life and he gave them both his very best.

I am so proud of my late father.

Brig. Sawai Bhawani Singh, MVC, of Jaipur
2005

PROLOGUE

JAIPUR, 29 MARCH 1949

A despondent V.P. Menon, the co-architect of the merger of kingdoms with India along with Heera Lal Shastri, the chief minister designate of the United States of Great Rajputana, drove back to Ram Bagh Palace from Sanganer Airport at 6 p.m., after a day-long wait. Sardar Vallabhbhai Patel, India's home minister was to have reached Jaipur by air for the swearing-in of the new government of Rajputana, the next day.

After Menon reached the Ram Bagh Palace, a frantic message was sent to Delhi. Delhi sent back word that Sardar Patel had left Delhi at 11 a.m. There was no further information, and the aircraft was incommunicado.

An anguished Menon queried, 'What if Patel has died?' After a pause he said, 'I will go to Delhi and get Jawaharlal Nehru to inaugurate Rajputana if required, but the event will not be postponed.' Menon had orchestrated the tortuous negotiations and understood the importance of the occasion and the consequences involved. The call was too close.

To their eternal relief, Patel arrived at Ram Bagh Palace at ten minutes past midnight. Apparently, his aircraft had developed a snag and had been forced to land near Alwar. A car had been commandeered to complete the journey to Jaipur.

On arrival, he immediately called a meeting of the prominent four in the Congress echelon—Heera Lal Shastri, Jai Narayan Vyas, Manik Lal Verma, and Gokul Bhai Bhatt— to take stock of the situation and make plans. It had already been agreed that the former two would join the new Cabinet while the latter two would handle the organization.

CITY PALACE, 30 MARCH 1949, 9.00 A.M.

There was an air of festivity in City Palace. In the *Sharbata* (hall of audience with the king) were gathered the who's who of royalty in Rajputana, the prominent members of the Congress, including the powerful four, and other dignitaries. This was the first time since City Palace had come into existence that men without turbans had been permitted entry and accorded the status of guests. For the apprehensive rulers, the mood was sombre. The excitement was affected, and the strain was showing. They might as well have been at a funeral.

Menon was awaiting Patel, when the agitated voice of Manik Lal Verma was heard. Verma was apparently unhappy with his seat in the second row. Sir V.T. Krishnamachari, the prime minister of Jaipur and the master of ceremonies, tried to pacify Verma. Heera Lal Shastri, the chief minister designate, chipped in to no avail.

Sardar Vallabhbhai Patel, Maharaja Sawai Man Singh Bahadur of Jaipur, and Maharao Bhim Singh, His Highness of Kota, entered the hall for the swearing-in. Maharaja Sawai Man Singh Bahadur of Jaipur was to be the *Rajpramukh*, Maharao Bhim Singh the *Up-rajpramukh* and Heera Lal Shastri, the chief minister.

With a short crisp announcement, Maharaja Sawai Man Singh was called upon to take the oath of office.

Sawai Man Singh, dressed immaculately, got up to take the oath as the first Rajpramukh of the United State of Rajputana (Rajasthan).

'I, Sawai Man Singh of Jaipur, hereby swear in the name of God that I ...'

However, even before the arrival of Sawai Man Singh, an agitated Manik Lal Verma had left the palace. Efforts by Gokul Bhai Bhatt, Paliwal, Daulatmal Bhandari, and Sidhraj Dhadda to persuade him to return had failed. The tryst with destiny and democracy was apparently not a bed of roses. The opponents of regency (they used to call it autocracy) were stunned. They shuddered at the prospect of a fragile democracy in the hands of those who could be provoked by a mere seating arrangement![1] Is this what *inqalaab* (revolution) meant? Was this the pot of gold at the end of the rainbow? Did they struggle and sacrifice for this change? From autocracy to rulers with petty egos! The incident did not augur well for the new dispensation.

But, the heritage had irretrievably changed hands.

---

1 In his autobiography, *Pratyaksha Jeevan Shastra,* Heera Lal Shastri says that the cleavage heralded by Verma's departure continued to widen and the situation would never be the same again.

PALACE INTRIGUES AND ADOPTIONS

He was born a commoner. He died a commoner. But there was nothing common about the life of His Highness Saramad-I Rajaha-I Hindustan Raj Rajendra Maharaja Dhiraj, Lieutenant-General Sir Sawai Man Singh Bahadur the Second, G.C.S.I., G.C.I.E., Maharaja of Jaipur (b. 1911–d. 1970). He was the last ruler of the Kachhwaha clan of the Kshatriyas to exercise sovereignty over Jaipur, and presided over its merger with independent India on 30 March 1949. The merger brought to an end approximately a 1000 years of Kachhwaha rule at Amber (Jaipur).

Another significant event had taken place much before the merger. In 1880 the direct line of the Kachhwahas who had ruled for centuries had ended with the adoption of Kayam Singh of Isarda (later Madho Singh II), a 19-year-old sepoy in the Tonk infantry. Kayam Singh, the younger brother of Pratap Singh, the thakur of Isarda, was to return the favour: he would adopt Mor Mukut Singh of Isarda, who would be known as Sawai Man Singh II.

Kayam Singh was born in 1861 and ascended the throne at the age of 19 years. Obviously, he had neither organized education nor training for a task of such calling. Lord Curzon described Madho Singh II as 'old-fashioned, conservative, reluctant to move away from his own state, liberal in the distribution of his funds, intensely loyal to the queen and the British connection, averse to being too bothered or fussed over, but capable, if skilfully and sympathetically handled, of being guided where desired.'

Lord Curzon was not off the mark. Madho Singh II turned out to be highly indolent and superstitious. However, he did not impose his ignorance on his subjects and largely adopted a policy of *laissez faire*. Consequently, the state improved financially.

Despite being superstitious, Madho Singh II was the first Kachhwaha ruler to travel overseas for the coronation of King Edward VII in London, in 1902. The journey was on invitation from the king and had practically been a command. Madho Singh II had no option but to go. In fact, earlier the Raja of Khetri[1] had been banned from entering City Palace for having travelled overseas. To justify Madho Singh II's trip, therefore, there had to be much drama. Brahmins were consulted. Benedictions were bestowed on the king. After much religious ceremony, he sailed from Bombay in 1902 aboard a new ship, *Olympia*, which was chartered and modified to suit his needs. He took the idol of his deity Gopal and necessary supplies for four months, including two huge casks carrying the holy Ganges water. The casks are prominently displayed in City Palace even today. His stay in London made headlines, thanks to his baggage and his entourage.

The old maharaja was extremely religious, which added to his gullibility. He was under the influence of his courtier Khawas Bala Bakshji, a man of doubtful integrity, and Roop Rai, a favourite concubine.

It is rumoured that Roop Rai used to eavesdrop whenever Madho Singh II was with his favourite queen. After this queen died, Roop Rai used to claim that the late Her Highness appeared in her dreams and asked her to carry out certain tasks. Being aware of the actual conversation, she made a convincing case before Madho Singh II. Over time, Roop Rai polished this approach to obtain a vice-like grip on the maharaja. She would even tell the maharaja that the late Her Highness had promised to meet her again in her dreams and that if he wanted to send a message, Roop Rai would convey it to her. Madho Singh II had two morganatic sons, Ganga Singh and Gopal Singh, for whom he had great affection. Both died prematurely. Roop Rai pretended to be possessed of their souls. She would speak to the maharaja on their behalf and about Ganga Singh's disease in the other world and demand money for his treatment. On one occasion, she asked for money for the deceased Gopal Singh's marriage in heaven!

Madho Singh II being the first king to be adopted from outside the direct line of the Kachhwahas, caused a lot of heartburn in Jhilai, which considered itself the senior branch of the ruling family. Since Madho Singh II was 19 years old when Ram Singh II adopted him on his deathbed, protests, if any, are unrecorded. Consequently, the adoption of Mor Mukut Singh (Sawai Man Singh) had more than its fair share of intrigues.

Stories and theories about Man Singh's adoption are legion. Madho Singh II was not wanting in physical prowess. In fact, he was a man of a rather voracious sexual appetite, with five queens and almost 40 *pardayats* (concubines).[2] They bore him over 50 children. According to one source, it was prophesied that if a son was born from Madho Singh II's loins to any of his queens, he (the king) would die within six months of the birth. Madho Singh II probably avoided begetting children from his queens for this reason. That adoption had become unavoidable engendered fervent hopes in different quarters and threw up the very first question: would the person to be adopted have to be from Jhilai?

Initially, Madho Singh II had suggested adopting someone other than Mor Mukut Singh. The name of this person, believed to be of his morganatic son Gopal Singh, was conveyed to Viceroy Harding in a sealed envelope in 1916. However, Gopal Singh died in early 1920. Soon Madho Singh II wrote to His Excellency, stating that the person whose name had been enclosed in the envelope had died, and he wanted to change the name.

The impending adoption became a hot topic of discussion and it was impossible to keep any secret in the durbar. Once it was obvious that Jhilai would be given a go by in the race for adoption, strenuous efforts began in the search for an heir. The thakur of Jhilai, in fact, went to the extent of making a formal representation to the British Government. Bikaner backed Jhilai, to the hilt. The British evaded the issue, saying they were unaware of the maharaja's plans. Bikaner wrote to Chelmsford voicing concerns about overlooking Jhilai. Madho Singh II, aware of the lurking dangers, also wrote to Chelmsford requesting that the nomination not be leaked out since the situation in Rajputana was such that 'publicity is sure to give rise to intrigues which may endanger my life.' About the delay in carrying out the adoption ceremony (probably because of the prophecy), he assured Chelmsford that his nomination was fully in conformation with the traditions and established usage of Jaipur. He wrote again to seek assurance and confirmation that his wishes would be

carried out. Chelmsford pressed the maharaja to go ahead
with the adoption immediately and publicly. Madho Singh II
was apprehensive of the objections that would surely be raised
against his nomination after his death. Even Chelmsford said
that were such a situation to come to pass, the government
would have no option but to take heed of the objections.

Mor Mukut Singh, the second son of Sawai Singh, the
thakur of Isarda, was born on 21 August 1911. His father was
not highly educated, but he was a shrewd man who doubled
the income of his *thikana* within his lifetime. Isarda had to
pay to Jaipur Rs 40,000 per year as tribute at that time. Mor
Mukut had one elder brother, Bahadur Singh, and three
sisters. Until the age of eight they lived in Isarda, riding
bullock carts, playing local games, and indulging in every
activity that the children of a village thakur could.

Sawai Singh had two sisters. One was married to the
Maharaja of Kota. The other was married to Major General
Apji Sir Onkar Singh of Palaitha. Since there were no facilities
for education in Isarda, Sawai Singh sent both his sons,
Bahadur and Mor Mukut, to Kota to be educated. In Kota,
they stayed in Palaitha House. Pandit Harihar Nathji Sukhia
was their private tutor.

That Madho Singh II was looking towards Isarda to choose
a successor was no secret. Photographs of both the sons of the
thakur of Isarda had already been called for by no less a
person than Roop Rai, Madho Singh II's favourite concubine.
Whether the elder son Bahadur Singh should be adopted in
preference to Mor Mukut was hotly debated. Both the boys
were called in person. There are many versions of how Mor
Mukut was selected over Bahadur Singh. One was Madho
Singh II's belief that the eldest son of a *jagirdar* should not be
adopted. The second was that the reports of Bahadur Singh's

character were not very encouraging. An earlier incident exhibiting Mor Mukut's character also seems to have impressed Madho Singh II. Once, Mor Mukut had teased an elephant. Finally the elephant had charged at him. However, the boy had not shouted for help. Whether he wanted to avoid getting caught making mischief or took pride in not acknowledging fear publicly, is difficult to say. Both reasons reflected well on the lad.

Gur Nidhan Singh, an old timer, had another incident to narrate. Madho Singh II had gone to Indergarh (Sawai Madhopur). Isarda is located close by. Hence, the thakur of Isarda, Sawai Singh, who was Madho Singh II's real nephew went to pay obeisance with both his sons—Bahadur Singh and Mor Mukut Singh. Madho Singh II was sitting on a carpet with some courtiers and asked the boys to sit down. Sawai Singh and Bahadur Singh sat down but Mor Mukut Singh could not find a place to sit. He innocently complained to the king that there was no place for him. Madho Singh II called Mor Mukut and made him sit on his lap. The act was prophetic.

Yet another version talks of how both the brothers were waiting in the durbar to present *nazar* to Madho Singh II.[3] The younger one, Mor Mukut, got bored of waiting and pocketed the coin. His cheekiness appealed to the maharaja. As Rajmata Gayatri Devi remarks in her memoirs in *A Princess Remembers*, they were given an audience in City Palace, and each boy held out in his cupped hands, in a ceremonial way, a gold coin, to be accepted by the ruler in acknowledgement of their allegiance. The Jaipur legend is that while Jai's brother stood, Jai, who was only 10, grew impatient at the maharaja's slowness in accepting the tribute, dropped his hands to the side and pocketed the gold coin. This so struck the maharaja as a sign of independence and character appropriate to a prince, that he took to adopting the younger boy.

However, Pandit Harihar Nathji Sukhia, the boys' tutor at Kota who had accompanied them from Kota to Jaipur for the first time for the interview, had a different version. In the words of Pandit Sukhia:

> After a month or so, news came from Isarda that both the Kanwar Sahibs with myself and Dhabhai Mangi Lalji of Isarda were to proceed to Jaipur and meet Khawas Bala Bakshji as early as possible. Accordingly, we left Kota for Jaipur and on our way picked up Dhabhai Mangi Lalji. We arrived in Jaipur and stayed at Khawas Bala Bakshji's residence, and he informed us that both the Kanwars of Isarda should present themselves at the Khasa Naka, as commanded by Maharaja Shri Sawai Madho Singhji. Accordingly, we four used to go to the Khasa Naka (Sharbata) and sit there for an hour or so every evening, awaiting our chance for an audience. This daily visit continued for six days. On the seventh day, as luck would have it, Khawas Bala Bakshji came out from within with commands from His Highness Shri Maharaja Sahib Bahadur that all four of us should move to Naya Naka to present nazar to Shri Hazur Sahib. The two brothers proceeded side by side towards the Naya Naka, I and Dhabhai Mangi Lalji walking behind them. The moment we entered the small room, where Hazur Sahib was sitting, both the brothers stood before His Highness side by side and extended their hands to present nazars to Hazur Sahib, who looked first at Kanwar Bahadur Singhji and then at Kanwar Mor Mukut Singhji and then picked up the nazars after about 15 seconds. After a month, the long-awaited action of His Late Highness Maharaja Sawai Madho Singhji regarding the selection of an heir-apparent to the Gaddi of Jaipur State, was finally taken.

There were many factors that led to the rejection of Jhilai. According to the grapevine, when Madho Singh II was adopted, it had been pledged to Jhilai that it would not be overlooked the second time. However, there is no evidence of such an understanding. Even if such an assurance had been given, there were reasons enough in the changed context for Madho Singh II to ignore the assurance. Gordhan Singh, the ruler of Jhilai, was 36 years old and not on the best of terms with the Maharaja of Jaipur. Madho Singh II, therefore, concluded that Gordhan Singh would not look after Madho Singh II's mother, widows, concubines or his children after his death. Gordhan Singh himself had been adopted from Bikaner, and his wife was the niece of the Maharaja of Bikaner. Madho Singh II, therefore, surmised that this could compromise the interests of Jaipur State. In addition, Gordhan Singh's adoption would have left Jhilai vacant. According to yet another story, Madho Singh II dreamt that a deity had sent Mor Mukut Singh to him.

It should be noted that Mor Mukut Singh was the grandson of Madho Singh's real brother, Pratap Singh, from Isarda. It was rumoured that courtier Khawas Bala Bakshji and Roop Rai had more than a fair share of say in preparing the ground in favour of Isarda. Some sources even aver that Khawas Bala Baksh and Roop Rai had orchestrated the entire adoption exercise. Tota Ram Swami was the advocate of Isarda. Through his good offices, Khawas Bala Baksh and Roop Rai were both persuaded to use their influence with Madho Singh II to adopt Mor Mukut Singh. This, of course, came with a price. But Khawas Bala Baksh and Roop Rai were the linchpins. Realizing that Madho Singh II's end was near, both indulged in intrigue and embezzlement. Khawas Bala Baksh had managed to catapult himself to such a lofty position that, later, it became difficult even for the British government (during the minority council of Man Singh) to ignore him. He had been promoted to the rank of a noble by Madho Singh II and was the head of the *Kapat Dwara* (private treasury). The Britishers referred to Roop Rai as the 'female Rasputin' and 'that pestilential woman'. Another person who was inexplicably close to the maharaja was the wife of Ramnath Seth of Beawar, popularly called the 'Sethani'.

Jhilai was carrying out a signature campaign against Isarda with the open support of Bikaner. Madho Singh II was weak and debilitated. The situation was so confusing that some people, in fact, started presenting *nazar* to the thakur of Jhilai. Madho Singh II was furious. He convened an open durbar on 12 March 1921. Despite being ill, he gave a speech informing everyone that he had chosen a successor according to tradition. Even though he did not reveal the name of the successor, he called upon everyone present (even those otherwise forbidden to enter City Palace had been called) to sign a document acknowledging his right and power to adopt anyone he pleased in keeping with tradition. For effect, he specified that this was not an order, and that no cognizance would be taken of those who did not sign the document.

According to the famous diarist Amar Singh,[4] the durbar continued for three days. Most people came and signed. There were two prominent exceptions, Chomu and Diggi. After the ceremonies, Madho Singh II dismissed Chomu from the council of ministers on the grounds of being disloyal. Moreover, Chomu and Diggi were barred from entering the palace. So much for the king keeping his word. Later, there were rumours that Chomu and Diggi were planning to eliminate Madho Singh II.

The three-day durbar and the signature campaign did not seem to come to much. Adoption became unavoidable. The options before Madho Singh II were limited to either going ahead with the adoption and neutralizing the ominous prophecy or leaving the name in the envelope and inviting almost certain objections to his choice. The prospect of Jhilai coming to Jaipur after all this acrimony was disconcerting. The fate of all he would leave behind was a constant worry. The old king opted to heed the prophecy and go ahead with the adoption.

It was in such times of confusion that Mor Mukut Singh was smuggled out from Kota. On 21 March 1921, Captain McCaughnegy, the political agent of Kota, had to take the charge of Tonk and Hadoti from Colonel Ben. The meeting was organized at Devli, and the Captain was asked to bring Mor Mukut Singh with him. From Devli, Colonel Ben brought him towards Jaipur. Sir Charles Cleveland received them 21 miles off Jaipur. The initial plan was to reach at 9 p.m., but the party reached City Palace at 5.30 p.m. Rai Bahadur Babu Avinash Chandra Sen, Rai Bahadur Khawas Bala Baksh and Home Minister Sir Purohit Gopinath received them. Khawas Bala Baksh took the future king and handed him over to the ladies in the zenana. Mor Mukut Singh was placed under the care of Maji Sahiba Rathore Ji,[5] the first wife of Ram Singh II. The entire mission was kept a secret. Ostensibly, there was a threat to his life and to that of Madho Singh II.

Madho Singh II adopted Mor Mukut Singh formally on 24 March 1921. He was rechristened Sawai Man Singh. *Nazars* were presented to the maharaja and the new maharaj kumar. The function had all the pomp and pageantry of a royal celebration.

The viceroy was informed and a request was made to formally sanction the adoption. According to Amar Singh, there were two to three parties every night for weeks together. Now even Chomu and Diggi were keen to sign on the dotted line. However, the viceroy had not yet confirmed the adoption. Bikaner continued with the dauntless fight for Jhilai, urging the British not to accede to such an undesirable course of action. Bikaner even threatened to go to England and seek an interview with the secretary of state. Delay in confirming validity added fuel to many speculations, although the delay was occasioned because of the change of viceroys. The new viceroy, Lord Reading, confirmed the adoption on 21 April 1921 and sent the *kharita*[6] to Jaipur on 10 June for the official durbar.

His Excellency Lord Reading while replying to the letter of His Highness Madho Singh II wrote in his *kharita*:

> I have examined the case with great care in consultation with my advisors and have decided that the claim of the thakur of Jhilai cannot be sustained and that the adoption made by Your Highness is in accordance with Hindu Law and the custom of your race. I have, therefore, great pleasure in informing Your Highness that the Government of India recognizes and confirms your adoption of Kunwar Mor Mukat Singh, now renamed Maharaja Kumar Man Singh, as your heir and successor to the Gaddi of Jaipur.
>
> I fervently hope that Your Highness' action in adopting this boy will bring peace and happiness to yourself and I am confident that he will follow the example of Your Highness and your predecessors in loyalty and devotion to the British Crown.

In recognition of the adoption, Sir R.E. Holland, agent to the governor general in Rajputana, delivered a speech in the adoption durbar. Here are some excerpts[7].

> Forty years have elapsed since an agent to the governor general, Sir Edward Bradford, presented to Your Highness in this hall, with due ceremony, a *kharita* from His Excellency the Viceroy announcing the recognition and confirmation of your succession to the Gaddi of Jaipur. By His Excellency the Viceroy's command, I have delivered to Your Highness today a *kharita* of equal moment recognizing and

confirming the adoption by Your Highness of Maharaj Kumar Man Singh as your successor. The adoption marks the culmination of Your Highness's long and benevolent rule, since by it you have grafted upon the ancient tree of Jaipur a young and vigorous shoot... But though Your Highness has grown grey in the toilsome service of a ruler for his people and in devotion to the cause of His Majesty the King Emperor, there is yet one other work to be achieved for the good of your people before you let slip the reins of government from your hands; and that work, which you have inaugurated with the adoption of a son and an heir, is to impart to this boy from your own wisdom and experience the knowledge and training which will enable him to discharge successfully the duties of his magnificent inheritance.

Concurrently with his training in Rajput thought and sentiment and in all the lore with which Your Highness can endow him, it will be necessary for Man Singh, in due course, to assimilate Western culture and knowledge which are now so essential faith: he will be fitted, not only to turn good account for his people all that is profitable in European knowledge and discovery, but also to play his part as an ally and helper of the King Emperor under whose sway the destinies of India are developing.

The character, disposition and qualities of the youth whom Your Highness has chosen as your adopted son and successor are such as to justify the brightest auguries for his future and the highest hopes for the destinies of this great State under his guidance. I trust that Your Highness may be spared to witness, in the fullness of time, the unfolding of the flower from the bud in which it is hid, and I pray that, as a ruler, Man Singh may rival and surpass the traditions of your illustrious predecessor after whom you have named him, Maharaja Man Singh, contemporary and friend of the Emperor Akbar.

I hope that he may never be called upon, as Man Singh was, to take sword in hand in defiance of the State of Jaipur or in the service of the King Emperor. But even though princes no longer find occasion to give such impassioned and heroic expression to their devotion and loyalty as in old days, yet the labours which they are called upon to perform are in some ways more strenuous and exacting than ever before.

It was a formal durbar of speeches of felicitations, thanksgiving, and good wishes. His Highness responded:

> I thank His Excellency the Viceroy for the *kharita* which you have today delivered to me by his command and I thank you for coming here and for your encouraging and most eloquent words. I am glad that the great British Government speaking through His Excellency the Viceroy and yourself have recognized and confirmed my adoption of a son and successor and thereby set the final seal upon my act of State which was intended by me to be right and in accordance with the *Dharma Shastras* and the customs of my House. This act of mine was conceived and carried out, after the most earnest deliberation, for the good of my state, for the happiness and security of my beloved subjects and in the humble service of the God of my ancestors and of myself.
>
> You have been pleased to say that the character, disposition, and qualities of my adopted son, Man Singh, justify the brightest auguries for his future and the highest hopes for the destinies of his state under his guidance. I am pleased and proud that you have, by forming this favourable judgment, endorsed my choice, and I am also glad that it has been received with equal approbation by my peers and by the humblest and highest of my subjects.

His Imperial Majesty, the King Emperor, sent a telegram with the following message on the adoption:

> I cordially congratulate you upon the selection of Kunwar Mor Mukut Singh as your heir. To both of you I send my sincere good wishes and look forward to the continued prosperity of yourself and your State.

The secretary of the state joined the stream of people sending their felicitations:

> My heartiest congratulations upon your adoption of Mor Mukut Singh. I hope you may be long spared in happiness and health and that your successor may be destined to prove worthy of following Your Highness in the position Your Highness

worthily filled. Please accept my sincere good wishes for your welfare.

The adoption had finally been formalized.

---

1   The Raja of Khetri was a highly educated person, interacting and corresponding regularly with the likes of Swami Vivekananda, and was one of the three members of the constituent assembly from Rajputana.

2   Madho Singh II had one daughter from his first wife; she was betrothed to Maharana Bhupal Singh of Udaipur. She died when she was thirteen. Subsequently, the maharana got married to the Achrol Thakur's daughter. Madho Singh II did not like this (What a fall! Jaipur to Achrol!) and, consequently, refused to provide silver utensils and other help for the marriage, which would ordinarily have been made available.

3   *Nazar* is a custom where the nobles affirm their loyalty to the maharaja by approaching the throne one by one, kneeling down and holding out a gold coin in their cupped hands, one resting on the other. The maharaja takes the coin if he wants to accept the nazar.

4   Major General Rai Bahadur, thakur Amar Singh of Kanota was in the ringside seat for most of the period mentioned. He used to write his personal diary regularly. His dairies have now been compiled and published by Oxford University Press, India, in 2000, titled *Reversing the Gaze*.

5   According to the custom, the queens and dowager queens used to be referred to by their maiden surname. Maji Sahiba Rathore Ji was the daughter of Maharaja Takhat Singh Ji of Jodhpur.

6   A formal order of the viceroy.

7   The entire text of the *kharita* and speeches are given in the Jaipur Album kept with the HH Sawai Man Singh II Museum Trust.

Mor Mukat Singh, the younger of the two sons of Sawai Singh, the Thakur of
Isarda, was adopted by Sawai Madho Singh II, the Maharaja of Jaipur,
and rechristened Sawai Man Singh II.

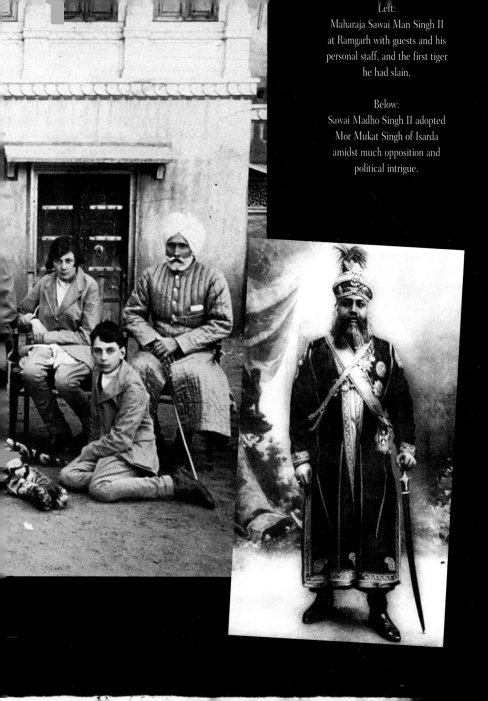

Left:
Maharaja Sawai Man Singh II
at Ramgarh with guests and his
personal staff, and the first tiger
he had slain.

Below:
Sawai Madho Singh II adopted
Mor Mukat Singh of Isarda
amidst much opposition and
political intrigue.

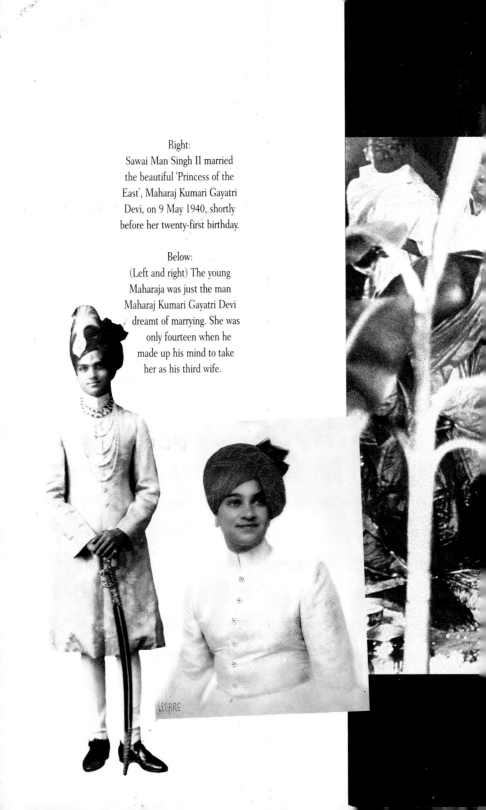

Right:
Sawai Man Singh II married
the beautiful 'Princess of the
East', Maharaj Kumari Gayatri
Devi, on 9 May 1940, shortly
before her twenty-first birthday.

Below:
(Left and right) The young
Maharaja was just the man
Maharaj Kumari Gayatri Devi
dreamt of marrying. She was
only fourteen when he
made up his mind to take
her as his third wife.

Right:
The Maharaja on a field trip in
the State of Jaipur.

Below:
This portrait shows Sawai Man
Singh II in full uniform of the
Sawai Man Guards.

Right:
(Left to right) Maharaja Prithvi Singh of Baria, Rao Raja Abhay Singh, Maharaja Sawai Man Singh II of Jaipur and Rao Raja Hanut Singh made up the formidable Jaipur Polo Team.

Below:
Under the able leadership of the polo-playing Maharaja,the Jaipur Polo Team won all the tournaments when it went abroad in 1933.

Left:
Sardar Vallabhbhai Patel arrives in Jaipur for the swearing-in ceremony of Sawai Man Singh II as the Rajpramukh of the United States of Rajputana in 1949.

Below:
The Rajpramukh with Pandit Jawaharlal Nehru (centre), Morarji Desai (right) Jagjivan Ram (extreme left), in Jaipur. In 1956 he received three letters—from the President of India, the Prime Minister and the Home Minister—apprising him that he was no longer Rajpramukh of Rajputana.

Left:
The Maharaja and Maharani
with the four sons, Bubbles,
Joey, Jagat and Pat. This family
portrait was taken in London.

Below:
Maharaja Sawai Man Singh II
and Maharani Gayatri Devi
had just one child, a son
they named Jagat.

Right:
The Maharaja at a durbar
in the City Palace with the
thakurs seated in order of
their importance.

Below:
The Maharaja flanked
by Maharani Gayatri Devi
and his eldest son
Sawai Bhawani Singh.

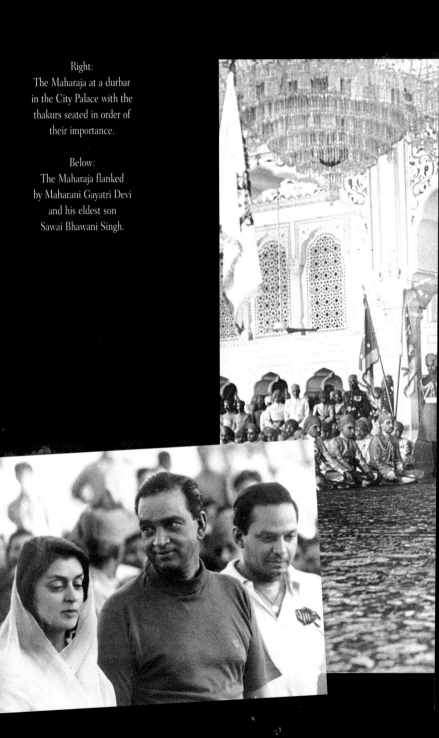

Maharaja Sawai Bhawani Singh, the present ruler of Jaipur, had an illustrious career in the Army before becoming a successful hotelier. He has carried forward the rich legacy of his polo-playing father.

TRAINING TO BE KING

The thorny issue of adoption having been settled, Madho
Singh II concentrated on providing proper education to
the maharaj kumar. He used to discuss the matter at length
with his medical advisor, Sir James Robert, and Sir Charles
Cleveland. Surprisingly, all along, the old king kept the
maharaj kumar close to him. In January 1922, Madho Singh II
went on a pilgrimage to Indergarh (Sawai Madhopur). The
maharaj kumar and Roop Rai, accompanied him. This ill-
advised and ill-timed visit was allegedly organized by Roop Rai,
ostensibly to get the maharaja cured by a sage with healing
powers. They stayed in tents for days on end in pouring rain. It
was a trying time, since the maharaja was not in the best of
health. There was also apprehension that the maharaja would
not return alive. If he died at any place away from Jaipur, it
would be embarrassing for the state. In fact, Patterson, the
new resident in Jaipur had agreed that in the event of the
maharaja's death he 'would inform the government by
telegram… and treat His Highness alive, until he died
officially in the palace'. Fortunately, the maharaja returned to
Jaipur alive. According to the agent to the governor general,

R.E. Holland's report to Delhi, two women servants had disappeared! It is alleged that Roop Rai never wanted Madho Singh II to return to Jaipur alive, so that she could decamp with the large amount of jewellery that she had carried to Indergarh. Rumour has it that Roop Rai had sent the women servants off with the jewellery.

These apparently minor incidents are indicative of the intrigues and circumstances prevalent at that time.

Madho Singh II died in September 1922. Since Sawai Man Singh was barely 11 at the time, a minority council was formed. Such was the situation that Cleveland found himself powerless against the potent combination of Roop Rai, Khawas Bala Baksh, the swarm of ladies, and eunuchs (there were a total of 5,000) living in the zenana. The eviction of Roop Rai was an operation in itself. She declined a polite request to vacate. Eunuchs were sent to use force, when she and her camp (she had a 100 women with her) drew swords. However, subsequently she was persuaded to leave by the *Laljis* (the sons of the maharaja through their concubines). Considering the odds against her, she relented. A search of her quarters in the palace yielded Rs 3 lakh in cash, 50 swords and a large quantity of liquor, spirit, and even poison. Khawas Bala Baksh was put in the prison after a protracted process and the Rajrana of Dhrangadhra was called and inducted into the Cabinet, primarily to restore some semblance of control in the zenana. The Cabinet carried out a thorough search of the palace including the stores. Government promissory notes and sovereigns were found tucked away in strange, apparently abandoned places.

A young Man Singh from a rural background had once been smuggled into the zenana, into this background. He was to recall that time as 'the unhappiest period of his life'. None of

his family except his favourite sister (the youngest, Chand[1])
used to visit him.[2] There were about 50 morganatic children of
Maharaja Madho Singh II living in the zenana, playing
frivolous games like cards and *chaupar* and doing little else.

Surprisingly, the first thing that Madho Singh II did on —
adopting Man Singh was to send an emissary to the regent of
Jodhpur, Sir Pratap, arranging for Man Singh's marriage to two
of the princesses (his aunt and niece) from Jodhpur.
Simultaneously, the morganatic children of Madho Singh II
were to be married to their corresponding counterparts of the
Maharaja of Jodhpur and Sir Pratap.[3]

The aunt, Marudhar Kanwar, the sister of Maharaja
Ummaid Singh of Jodhpur was 22 years of age and was 12
years older than Man Singh. The niece, Kishore Kanwar, was
the daughter of Maharaja Sumer Singh, the elder brother of
Maharaja Ummaid Singh. She was five years younger than
Man Singh. Despite the disapproval of the British, Man Singh
was formally betrothed to both the princesses on 31 December
1921. He was a little over 10 at that time. A vain effort was
even made to repudiate the betrothal. Man Singh was married
to Marudhar Kanwar on 30 January 1924, one and a half year's
after the death of Madho Singh II. The *barat* was sent from
Amber in a train and arrived in the morning at Jodhpur to a 19-
gun salute. The maharajas exchanged *nachhrawal*, a customary
form of welcome and greetings. The groom's procession took
two hours to reach the fort, and the celebrations continued for
about a week.

A 'will' had been left by Madho Singh II to exclude Chomu,
Diggi, and Jhilai from the palace as well as from the Cabinet.
However, the old guard was too well entrenched. The 'will' was
given a go by. Within a short while this group got rid of
Cleveland from the presidency of the Minority Council (he

was replaced by R.I. Glancy), and of Dharangadhra, who had been specially inducted into the Cabinet for the smooth functioning and control of the zenana.

A month after Madho Singh II's death, Sir James Robert started a school at Ram Bagh Palace, where he himself did most of the teaching. Twenty boys from noble and other families were selected. J.W.C. Mayne—principal of the Chief's College at Rajkot, an institution of some repute—was brought in and was appointed the deputy guardian. J.K. Atal (later to be Man Singh's finance minister) was one of the boys selected.

The basic traits of Man Singh's personality were evident even at this stage. In the words of Atal:

> As I was the youngest and perhaps the smallest boy at school, Maharaja Sahib, for reasons which I never found out, took me under his protection. When his own elder brother Bahadur Singh or any other bigger boy tried to bully me or harm me in any way, he would immediately rush up and protect me. I do not remember him ever beating any boy or being anything but kind, fair and gentle towards the young and old during those two years at Ram Bagh.

Later, the new maharaja was removed to Mount Abu following a Cabinet decision, because of a perceived threat to his life. There was strife in the higher echelons of the durbar. Whether Man Singh should be sent out of Jaipur at all was an issue that encouraged much debate. Sir James with whom Madho Singh II had consulted extensively regarding the maharaj kumar's education, insisted that his late Highness had always desired that the boy be educated in Jaipur. Sir James accordingly had planned to educate him along with the contemporary nobles, who would later be Man Singh's supporters in state matters. While education was important, safety was also vital. Due to inadequate infrastructure, education at Jaipur had already been discarded. Mayo College, Ajmer, seemed to be the most suitable and obvious answer. Even the ladies in the palace, including the Dadi Sahiba Rathore Ji (Ram Singh II's widow), agreed.[4]

It is generally believed that young Man Singh got his grounding in polo at Mayo. However, his cousin, a playmate at Kota, and later his private secretary (and still later, home secretary and development secretary), Dalel Singh says:

> I may mention that it was during his stay at Kota that young Mor Mukut Singh Ji learnt his first lessons in the game of polo, and it was a matter of immense pride and gratification to those of us who had played with him in those days to see him later blossom forth into a polo player of international fame. The wooden dummy horse on which he practised his first polo strokes is still preserved at Kota.

When Man Singh went to Mayo, J.W.C. Mayne accompanied him. Lt. Col. C.C.H. Twiss became his guardian after Mayne left in July 1927. Mayne was very fond of Man Singh. His letter, written to Man Singh from Bombay—just before sailing to England—shows the bond they shared.

> My very dear Man Singh,
>
> You will get this letter after we have left you. Leaving you is just like leaving a son, and we shall miss you terribly. But, please God, we shall meet again before very long.
>
> I am sure that no guardian has ever had a nicer ward than I have had. You have never resented anything that I have done in my efforts to guide you, and my wife and I are very proud of you. We shall be a long way apart now but distance is nothing to the heart and mind and we shall often be together in spirit, for we shall often think and talk of you and Jaipur, and I feel you will do so of us.

If you understand 'Noblesse oblige' I have no fears for you—this and 'Ich dien' ('I serve'), the Prince of Wales's motto.

I am glad to say that you are 'princely' in many ways already, e.g., in your kindness to others, especially those lower in status than yourself and those less fortunate than you—this quality will make you [beloved]. Be 'princely' also in giving, for giving is far better than taking. The lame man at Abu will always bless you. Be 'princely' towards your people by protecting them and having no mercy on those nazims and tehsildars who rob and oppress them. This will make you beloved, and a maharaja who has not the love of his subjects is like an egg without a yolk or a ship without a rudder. Think well on this. (A ship without a rudder will soon be wrecked.)

You have been very kind to our children and they love you...

You are already 'princely' in your dignity and bearing: it is good for a prince to be a big man, I think. Think of your state a little daily and more as you get older. If you see anything you do not like, speak to the president about it when you see him. He will think all the more of you if he sees you interested.

Do not forget your prayers. I fear we all do this sometimes. I have always told you that Parameshwar has made you Maharaja of Jaipur: it was not just chance that took you away from Isarda. I am sure of this. And it was not just chance that sent me to be your guardian. This is a very sublime thought and like 'Noblesse oblige', will help you greatly. Col. Twiss will look after you well, I know. Trust him and continue to trust other real friends. We shall never forget you. God bless you and may he make you just the ruler that Jaipur wants.

Yours ever affectionately,
C. Mayne

At this point, Man Singh was not even permitted to visit his wife (First Her Highness) alone. An English woman always accompanied him. Amar Singh has noted in his diary that such a procedure was uncalled for and unwarranted, even if Man

Singh was only 14. First Her Highness detested this. She showed it, too.

In 1927, the police were trying to stop gambling in Jaipur. The campaign ignited protests. Shopkeepers refused to open their shops. First Her Highness went on a hunger strike in sympathy. She called officials and demanded that Man Singh be brought back from Mayo and be given full powers. Even though Amar Singh wrote that this protest had as much to do with the restrictions placed on the meeting between husband and wife as with the plight of citizens, there is no way this assumption could either be verified or presumed to be true.

While at Mayo, Man Singh used to correspond frequently with home minister Sir Purohit Gopinath, his teacher at Jaipur, Rai Suraj Narain Sharma, and his grandmother Dadi Sahiba Rathore. The letters to the former two used to be in English, whereas those to Dadi Sahiba were written in the Devnagari script and in the dialect that Man Singh used to speak at Isarda before his adoption. His letters to Dadi Sahiba show his simplicity and innocence. He would inform her of daily activities like celebrations on his birthday, about the six dogs he had, or about clearing the exams. He complained to his grandmother about why he was not called for her birthday and enquired if she was annoyed with him. The correspondence continued even when Man Singh was at Mount Abu and Ooty.

Dadi Sahiba Rathore expired on 11 June 1926. Man Singh was in Mount Abu and rushed to Jaipur for her funeral. It had been planned that her cortege would be taken through Gangauri Gate[5] and Brahmpuri. Arrangements were made accordingly. Man Singh rejected the plan immediately on arrival. He directed that Dadi Sahiba be given the same respect as was customarily accorded to the eldest queen.

Consequently, her funeral procession was taken through Tripolia Gate. He himself walked on foot and had his head tonsured contrary to custom. Man Singh was just 15 then. The traits exhibited by him at this age—his simplicity, independence, his devotion to the family, and his firmness of character—were to come to the fore again many more times.

Man Singh was nearly 18 when he left Mayo College. The principal of the school praised his skills at horsemanship and games and also found him capable of exercising authority even at this stage. He wrote: 'His development from a little boy to a big athletic young man is as much a testimony to his inherent good qualities as to the system under which he has been brought up. He was never brilliant at his school work, but at a subject in which he was interested, he showed himself quick-brained and intelligent.' For good measure, the principal added: 'I myself will miss his cheery personality.' Incidentally, Heera Lal Shastri, who was to be the chief minister of Rajasthan at the dawn of Independence, was one of his teachers at Mayo.

Man Singh passed his diploma examination from Mayo. After this, another debate ensued: should he be sent to England for further education? Patterson opposed the idea on the ground that a boy must be taught religion, and a prince must keep in touch with the religion of the state and with his people. Mayne, who had grown very fond of Man Singh, suggested that he be sent to England. Initially, Man Singh was unhappy with the idea of moving to England, but realizing that he was to stay with Mayne and would be a day scholar, he acquiesced.

First Her Highness was against his going abroad. She wrote a strong letter listing out the grounds on which he could not be sent. First, that Maharaja Madho Singh II had desired that

Man Singh be educated in Jaipur. Second, that the public as well as the family, including her brother, the Maharaja of Jodhpur, would not like him to be out of the state. Finally she pointed out the extraordinary expenses involved in overseas travel. Madho Singh II's visit during the coronation was cited as an example. L.W. Reynolds, agent to the governor-general— who became the president of the Minority Council in 1924— also objected to Man Singh being sent to England. He feared that the subjects would take it as a deliberate step to distance the maharaja from them. He feared that First Her Highness might desire to accompany the maharaja.

However, all opposition was overcome, and Man Singh sailed from Bombay in July with Colonel Twiss and his elder brother Bahadur Singh. It was during this journey that Man Singh commenced correspondence with another 'Man Singh' of Barwara, who was four years younger. The maharaja had taken a fancy to the younger Man Singh, when he had once stopped at Barwara *en route* to Jaipur to accept *nazars* from the young boy and his family. The maharaja later nicknamed him Rabbit. He wrote to him from the ship.

My dear Baby,

It was sad saying goodbye to you in Jaipur. I do wish you could have come with me, but never mind. You will be able to do that in the future.

We saw no land for four days, which was rather awful. We reach Aden tomorrow. I hope you are working hard at your studies.

With best wishes,

Yours ever,
Man Singh

Man Singh's state of mind can be gathered over various spans of his lifetime, from the letters he wrote to Rabbit. In October, he wrote from Woolwich. 'I wish you were here with me to enjoy London life. You must see London one day. It is simply charming.' The charm of London was to stay with Man Singh until his dying days. (In fact, Man Singh died there.) The contents of his letters were indications, *inter alia*, of a prince released from the straitjacket of formalities and intrigues at Jaipur.

It was during this time, that Man Singh got the nickname Jai (short for Jaipur). Whenever Jai was in Jaipur for a break, he had to attend to certain formal functions. Outside of the regal duties, Jai kept himself busy with sports. He went for his first tiger shoot in January 1926. It was a cropper. Jai shot his first tiger in May that year, and the event was considered important enough for the nobles to present *nazars* to Jai in the evening. Jai was not unduly fond of shikar himself. He used to host shikar parties for his guests but was 'almost reluctant' to join the shoot himself.

In England, Jai was having the time of his life. He had many amusements to fall back upon, and he was a remarkably good-looking man with an appealing personality. Besides, he was the maharaja of a famous state. He, therefore, appeared regularly in the gossip columns of newspapers, not only in London but in New York and Paris as well. Agent Reynolds pressed for his early return to India, so that the maharaja could be given a ringside view of his kingdom and receive administrative training before regal powers were vested in him. Jai was not keen to return and offered to get attached to a cavalry regiment for more training in 1931, but Reynolds put his foot down. He rationalized that the object of the training was to produce a good 'ruler', not a good 'cavalryman'.

Jai stayed at Woolwich for exactly one year. The commandant at Woolwich gave a favourable report about his training and participation in all the activities.

Jai was called back to Jaipur to receive on-the-job administrative training. Meanwhile, First Her Highness had given birth to Princess Prem Kumari, popularly known as Mickey, on June 1929 at Shimla. She was the first child to be born to the Queen of Jaipur in almost a 100 years. The birth was, therefore, celebrated with jubilation. The present His Highness Bhawani Singh was born at Jaipur on 22 October 1931, the first male heir in a 100 years.

When Jai had left Jaipur, Jaipur was gradually inching out of the slumber of Madho Singh II's period. Palace intrigues, power peddling, nepotism and undue state largesse were common practices. The place was still medieval. The maharaja's water used to be drawn from a special well outside the walled city and carried to the palace under an escort. Traffic would be stopped and the public, carrying anything overhead including an umbrella, had to put it down for fear of the shadow falling on the water. The perpetual wrangles over adoptions, betrothals, and inheritances continued. The literacy rate was 4 per cent. The old maharaja's will created problems in the administration of the State. He had directed the establishment of a Cabinet as well as a council. (The Cabinet was subsequently abolished in 1925.) The gates of the walled city used to be closed, for the night at 11 p.m. and would not open for anyone until daybreak. The business within the zenana, among the swarm of ladies, continued at its old pace. Everyone knew everyone else's business. Chomu, Diggi, and Jhilai were back into the reckoning and Jai did not yet have full powers. It was this kind of Jaipur that Jai returned to after training at Woolwich. Lord Erwin, the then viceroy finally invested Jai with full powers as Maharaja of Jaipur on 14 March 1931, B.J. Glancy, president of the Minority Council, wrote to Jai:

My Dear Durbar,

My wife and I are both very grateful to you for the kind letter of appreciation that you have sent us. I hated saying goodbye to you last night, and I was almost base enough to wish that your team would be knocked out of the polo tournament so that we might meet again at Bombay.

I claim very little credit myself for the success of the investiture functions, but everyone from the viceroy downward seem to have been most favourably impressed and I felt personally very proud of the splendid way you played your part from start to finish. I suppose that every government official relieves his feelings from time to time by cursing and abusing the Government of India, and I confess now that I said some hard things about them when I heard of their decision that your training from last October onwards was to be confined to the Jaipur State. I did not know you well in those days, I had never been responsible for anybody's training, and I had grave doubts as to my own capacity and as to how we would get on together. Well, I take back all those wicked words today. For my part, I could have wished for nothing better than the last six months, and the happiest days that my wife and I have spent in Jaipur.

One thing I hope is that, however far you may advance as time goes on, you'll always remain the same at heart—just the same as you are at present.

Yours very sincerely,
B.J. Glancy

At the investiture durbar, Jai spoke from the heart. He said, 'It will be my constant endeavour to strengthen this bond of affection (which binds the ruler and the ruled together) still

further as the years go on, to remember at all times that my
main concern in life must be the welfare of my subjects so that
my officers know that in carrying out their duties they may
always rely on my support and that my people may feel that
their loyalty is not in vain.'

Jai was not yet 20.

---

1 Chand was six years younger than Man Singh. Man Singh's wife Marudhar
Kanwar (known as First Her Highness)) used to feel lonely in City Palace. She
requested Man Singh's Isarda mother to let her keep Chand. The request was
granted and Chand was brought up by First Her Highness. Chand now 85, still
has a vivid memory of those times.

2 Before adoption, Mor Mukut had four siblings for company (one brother and
three sisters). Apprehending that he might feel lonely, Madho Singh II had given
instructions that every desire of Maharaj Kumar Man Singh should be fulfilled.
The maharaj kumar was, however, undemanding. Once while sitting with the
Laljis, he absent-mindedly said: 'Come, Chand, let us play.' This incident was
conveyed to Madho Singh II, who called Man Singh and asked him who Chand
was. On being asked if he wanted to meet her, Man Singh still made no demand.
He merely said, 'As Your Highness desires.' Consequently, instructions were given
to bring Chand to meet Man Singh whenever he desired.

3 It may be interesting to note that the Maharaja of Kishangarh had met Madho
Singh II in Chandra Mahal on 2 June 1921 with a proposal of his eldest daughter
for Man Singh. However, Madho Singh II ignored the offer. This was eight days
prior to the formal adoption durbar where the viceroy's *kharita* was to be read.

4 Mayo College, founded by Lord Elgin in the nineteenth century, is the Eton of the
East. Ram Singh II of Jaipur had donated a princely sum of rupees one and half
lakh for the school. The school was established to educate the princes and the
nobles of the 21 states of Rajputana. Each state had its own house. However,
when the rulers themselves came for their education, they would have a separate
house of their own. The nobles and princes were obviously allowed to bring
servants, horses and *sayees* (person who looks after the horses) according to their
rank and stature.

5 Jaipur city has seven gates: Chand Pol on the extreme west and Suraj Pol on the
extreme east, lying 3 kms apart. Jorawar Singh Pol (old name Dhruv Pol) lies on
the north; on the southern side there are four gates: Ajmeri Gate (Kishan Pol),
Naya Pol, Sanganeri Gate (Shiv Pol), and Ghat Gate. All gates used to be closed
at night and this practice continued till 1942. City Palace has six gates within the
complex—Udai Pol, Vijay Pol, Jai Pol, Ganga Pol, Amba Pol, and Ganesh Pol.
Between the City Palace gates and Jaipur City gates lay Gangauri Gate and
Tripolia Gate. The cortege of the king and the eldest queen used to be taken from
Tripolia Gate; Gangauri Gate was used for the others.

LIFE IN JAIPUR

Winston Churchill had served in India as a cavalry officer, in the 4th Hussars. In *My Early Life*, Churchill writes:

> We built a large tiled barn with mud walls containing stables for 30 horses. Our three butlers formed a triumvirate in which no internal dissension ever appeared, we paid an equal contribution into the pot and thus freed from the mundane cares, devoted ourselves to the serious purpose of life. This was expressed in one word—Polo.

Polo is a game played by two teams of four players each. It is played with a ball, which is bigger than a cricket ball, and sticks, both made of wood. There are two referees. The game comprises four *chukkas*, each lasting seven and a half minutes. The handicap in polo is exactly the reverse of that in golf. The higher the handicap, the better the player in the world of polo. At the beginning of a match, the handicap of the entire team is added up. The team with the lesser total is awarded a proportionate number of goals on the 'Board' before the game commences. This ensures that both teams are at par.

Jai was so fond of polo that it was almost an appendage to his name. His great enthusiasm for the sport won him fame and popularity the world over. In a way, he was best placed to pick up the skill as well as the passion for polo. He started playing polo while at Kota, at a very young age. He could afford the best of ponies and the best of care for them. After Kota, Mayo College was his cradle for polo, during his school years.

Jai's passion for polo translated into action immediately on his return from Woolwich. He began to put together a polo team to participate in the British tournaments. From then on, Jai's life was to be compartmentalized between India and abroad, with at least four months being spent overseas every year. The polo team that he had assembled was the most powerful ever. Rao Raja Hanut Singh, son of Sir Pratap Singh (three-time Regent of Jodhpur and a great favourite of Queen Victoria) and Rao Raja Abhay Singh were from Jodhpur. Raja Prithi Singh, a nephew of the Maharaja of Baria, completed the team of four. Jai and Hanut had handicaps of eight, Abhay and Prithi commanded handicaps of seven.

This team, which was to carve a niche for itself in the polo world, sailed for England in 1933 carrying their own polo stick maker, 39 horses and 51 people to look after them. They trained at Westonbirt for a month. The season commenced in May, when they beat the West of England team, but lost to Osmaston at Hurlingham. However, in the Ranelagh Open Cup in June, they beat Osmaston and beat them again in the Hurlingham Champion Cup. They went on to win the Roehampton Open. This was the first time ever that one team had won all the three open championships within one year. The young maharaja was already popular in England and a dash of glamour was attached to every act of his. The lack of experience in polo added a fascination to this royal team. Even the most conservative papers eulogized its achievements. The team went on to win the King's Coronation Cup at Ranelagh, the Prince of Wales Empire Cup at Hurlingham, the Open and Senior cups at Dunster and the Rugy Challenge Cup. This was a feat never to be repeated.

The passion of the maharaja was infectious. When Man Singh returned to India, the army-backed polo club at Jaipur was abuzz with activity. When Man Singh was in Jaipur, his time would be taken up by two and a half hours of polo almost every afternoon. That was followed by bridge at the Jaipur Club. Jai was not a hard drinker and usually drank only champagne. A painful hangover in his young days pre-empted further adventures on this score. He would carry his champagne, whenever there was apprehension that the host might not be able to provide it. Whether at Ram Bagh Palace or at the Officer's Mess of one or the other regiment, parties were usually a male affair. The women were invited only occasionally, when Jai's friends from England were visiting.

There is very little literature available on the relationship between Jai and his family. His older queen was 12 years his senior. There is no doubt that she was very popular with the public. Undoubtedly, she was a pious and religious lady who had had a very traditional upbringing. Whenever she travelled, she would be very magnanimous in distributing largesse. Her sister was married to the Maharaja of Rewa and was her closest confidante. There is indeed no doubt that she remained dignified and was respected by all, including Jai. She was far above any kind of controversy. Gayatri Devi, recollects her first meeting with her in Ram Bagh Palace at Jaipur, when Gayatri was 12 years old. She says in *A Princess Remembers*: 'She did not wear any make up or make any pretence to modernity, but her manners were regal and impeccable.'

In accordance with the betrothal held during the lifetime of Madho Singh II, Jai had also to marry the niece of his elder queen, who was known as Second Her Highness. Her name was Kishore Kanwar. The marriage took place in April 1932.

There was an interesting prelude to the marriage. According to Rajput custom, before the groom departs for his marriage, he sucks the breasts of his mother. In Jai's case Madho Singh II's fifth queen, Ma Sahiba Tanwar[1], was still alive, as was the rajmata. The custom required Jai to suck Ma*ji*'s breasts, but Jai sucked the breasts of his own mother from Isarda. This, some allege, caused a lot of heartburn and resentment in the royal household. Chand disputes this version saying that Ma Tanwar was a widow and a widow's active participation on such auspicious occasions is usually avoided. Therefore, this departure from convention was made with the consent of Ma Tanwar herself.

Second Her Highness was only 15 when she got married. According to Chand, even the Jodhpur family was not happy about the second marriage. However, the marriage had to be solemnized on the insistence of Second Her Highness's maternal uncle Ranjit Singh of Jamnagar. Second Her Highness exhibited a fiercely independent streak during the marriage ceremony itself. The newly weds are required to go to the temple. She insisted that a gun salute be fired in her honour before she left the palace, as well as when she returned. Rumour has it that someone scoffed at the idea and suggested, in bad humour, that soda bottles be opened. They would sound like a gun salute. But Second Her Highness was made of sterner stuff. The last-minute insistence by the bride resulted in gross delay in the official ceremonials. However, there was no escape. Amar Singh has recorded the event in his diary on 25 April 1932, which reads as below:

> After the marriage when Maharaja Sahib of Jodhpur decided not to give a gun salute to the second Maharani Sahib of Jaipur, she refused to attend any further ceremonies. HH Jaipur was upset and called me. When I went to Maharaja Sahib, he said, 'There is a problem.' I said, 'If you have more than one wife you will have problems.' He said he was serious and told me about the gun salute. I said, 'Tell Maharani Sahib gun salute will be fired and she should get ready for further ceremonies.' Maharaja Sahib said, 'How can I give this guarantee?' I said the gun salute will be fired from our guns brought from Jaipur. The Maharani Sahib would not know whether the Jodhpur guns or Jaipur guns fired. The gun salute was given accordingly and the problem was solved.

Even though the grapevine and the diary entry related to this incident were possibly exaggerated, there is no doubt that a controversy did take place. Second Her Highness never returned to Jodhpur after the marriage because her demand — for a gun salute in her honour as the Queen of Jaipur had not met with a favourable response. Learning of the incident, Maharaja Ganga Singh of Bikaner invited her and welcomed her with a 19-gun salute. Much later, HH Maharaja Ummaid Singh of Jodhpur relented on a special occasion. This event has also been recorded in the diary of Amar Singh. The entry of 29 October 1941 reads as below:

> Thakur Sahib Bhadrajun who has come with Maharaja Ajeet Singhji told me that Second Maharani Sahib is going to Jodhpur. She never went to Jodhpur after her marriage because Maharaja of Jodhpur would not give a gun salute from Jodhpur Fort on the ground that only the Patrani[2] was entitled. The other ground was that Maharani Sahib Jodhpur is not on good terms with the widow of Maharaja Sumer Singhji. Now, Maharaja Sahib is to celebrate his sons' and daughter's marriages which are fast approaching and Maharani

Sahib of Jodhpur wants the second Maharani Sahib of Jaipur to attend the same, as such Maharaja Sahib has agreed to give a gun salute on her arrival at Jodhpur.

First Her Highness initially stayed in City Palace but finding it cloistered, shifted to Khasa Kothi. She was favourably disposed towards Second Her Highness. However, as is wont in palaces, interested elements were trying to drive a wedge between the two. It was insinuated that Jai preferred Second Her Highness, as she was younger and prettier. Chand, who was brought up by First Her Highness, disputes all these stories as canards. She avers that the kind of bonhomie and cordiality that existed between Jai's wives is almost inconceivable. This was illustrated in an incident that took place immediately after the second marriage.

Before his marriage to Second Her Highness, Jai's breakfast used to be prepared by the maids of First Her Highness. After the second marriage, the maids of First Her Highness refused to prepare it, putting the onus on the maids of Second Her Highness. The latter being new, did not know what to do. When Jai came down in the morning, he found that his breakfast had not been prepared. The matter was investigated, and Jai complained to First Her Highness. First Her Highness, known for her even temper, lost it on this occasion. Her maids were dressed down and were warned with expulsion if such effrontery was repeated. The incident had a sobering effect on mischievous minds.

In another incident, the wife of General Amar Singh Ajairajpura and the wife of the thakur of Achrol came to meet Second Her Highness. They saw First Her Highness, but deliberately did not curtsy. The matter was reported to Jai through Chand. Jai summoned the *thikanedars* the next day. He warned them that a repetition of such an incident would result in severe punishment, including forfeiture of the *thikana* and expulsion from Jaipur State. Such firm reaction from Jai nipped insidious designs and conveyed a clear message.

As per custom, the senior maharani conducts puja on the festival of Teej and Gangaur. After the marriage of Second Her Highness, First Her Highness handed over this task to Second Her Highness. Chand recollects being instructed by Jai Dada (elder brother) to be extremely careful and make sure that she did not convey the conversations or stories between the two to each other. Jai was a mature man and he ensured decorum.

Even though Jaipur had changed considerably since the days of Madho Singh, it was still a medieval place where life could get monotonous. Jai believed in living life to the full. He, therefore, welcomed every opportunity to go abroad. It saved Jai from the drudgery of a maharaja's routine in India. Quentin Crewe[3] writes: 'Jai's visits to England became an essential part of his life. It is not hard to imagine the attraction that England must have had for him. While it was delightful to be a maharaja in India, it had many disadvantages, the continuous squabbling, the unending intrigues, and the fathomless depths of sycophancy. The ever-present threat of British interference, the steady stream of favour seekers and once again the ultimately hollow quality of power were exacting and demanding.'

Jai's visits to England were regular since his coming of age and were interrupted only by World War II. The visits were purposed for entertainment and polo. These trips would also include forays into the countryside of Europe and even shooting parties in Romania and Austria.

Ram Bagh Palace grew in size in 1936 after Joey's birth. A zenana wing was added. After the new additions everyone shifted from Khasa Kothi to Ram Bagh Palace. A dining hall

(planned in London) was also added. The First and Second
Her Highness had two guestrooms each, in addition to their
own rooms. One of the guestrooms of First Her Highness had
a permanent occupant, Chand. The children Mickey,
Bubbles, Joey, and Pat had their governesses and the nursery
to themselves. The siblings were brought up together. As Joey
says, 'We didn't know who our mother was till we grew
up.' Shifting to Ram Bagh Palace had an added advantage.
Second Her Highness could play badminton and ride in the
zenana wing.

The requirements of the steady stream of visitors during
winter also dictated the changes at Ram Bagh. The staff of the
maharaja was trained to look after the guests. Every morning
the guests used to be asked about their choice of activities for
the day. The options were riding, sight-seeing, swimming or
shooting. Each event was meticulously planned and catered
for. The royal hunting grounds, zealously guarded, were
available for the guests. For others, tiger shooting had been
banned during Madho Singh's time itself. Morning shoots
used to be followed by picnic lunches. Afternoons were
occupied by polo, tennis or squash, followed by bridge at the
club in the evenings. Jai usually had a light lunch in the
zenana with his family. Afternoon tea times were almost
always spent with the children. Dinner would usually be out.
The timings for everyone else, except Jai were strict. If Jai was
to have a drink at some place and return for dinner, the dinner
would commence on his arrival, which could be as late as
2.30 a.m. Sir Robert Mortan, one of Jai's closest friends,
recalls that occasionally they would arrive to find the servants
sleeping. There were also frequent visits to other royal houses,
including Cooch Behar, for polo or pig-sticking.

Tiger shooting was a special occasion for which Jai's

selected guests used to be taken to Sawai Madhopur, a place where Jai had spent some time with the dying maharaja (Madho Singh II) immediately after his adoption. Although there was no paved road to this place, it was the most sought-after location for tiger shoots. Today, it is one of the most famous tiger sanctuaries of the world. It has been renamed Ranthambore National Park.[4] At the entrance of this reserve, there is a lake, with a beautiful cottage on the bank. Guests used to stay in luxury tents. These shoots were organized on a massive scale, with elephants, horses and a *haka* party. The maharaja and his friends used to sit on the machans. The *haka* party consisted of men making loud noises and moving in extended formation towards the machans from 8 to 10 kms away to goad the prey towards the waiting *shikaris*.

Even though Jai was a good shooter, he was not an enthusiastic hunter. He revelled more in the role of host. Col. Kesari Singh in his book *Hints on Tiger Shooting*, has said that Jai had one peculiar habit. An injured tiger or leopard is supposed to be lethal. Tracing and killing a wounded animal is always perilous. On such occasions, Jai would always go out himself, on foot, to kill the injured beast. Kesari wrote in his book:

> My present boss is a sportsman of international fame in polo. He is a good shot both with gun and rifle. After shooting a sufficient number of tigers, he is keener on giving tigers to his friends and guests than shooting them himself. The normal way of shooting a tiger from a machan does not now give him many thrills [sic]. He prefers to shoot the animal under conditions where there is an element of risk to himself. It is for this reason that he invariably goes after a wounded tiger or shoots it from the ground...

A good amount of hunting was available very close to Ram Bagh Palace (where Rajasthan University is situated today). In one incident, Narayan Singh Kanota (Col. Kesari Singh's father) and Sir Pratap hunted a panther that had taken refuge in the basement of Ram Bagh Palace.

Jai's weakness for his namesake Man Singh of Barwara (Rabbit) continued throughout his life. He had built a house for Rabbit with a special bar in the veranda to supply the last drink of the day (one for the road). Jai used to be in touch with not only Rabbit but also his wife, always warning her of Rabbit's weakness for the bottle. In one letter, he wrote: 'If you ever see him going the wrong way, try and stop him. I am only afraid for him taking to drinks, as you know that this weakness is there in all our family and we all at some time or the other succumb to it. Other things don't matter so much.' He frequently bailed out Rabbit, helping him in matters both financial and matrimonial:

Ram Bagh

13 Nov 1931

Rabbit my dearest,

Thank you ever so much for your letter. My dear babe, I have already taken steps towards excusing your debt and that will be perfectly all right. I did not tell you anything about it, as I wanted to make it a surprise for you. You are my dearest nephew and I would do anything in the world to help you. You can always rely on that.

Lots of love,

Yours ever
Man Singh

Most of the time, Rabbit was in trouble over various misdemeanours concerning his wife, his drinking, and his extravagances. Troubles recurred, but were always forgiven. Despite Jai's 'respect for cash', he was indulgent to his nephew. From Ooty he wrote: 'Do you want more money? If so send me a wire. Now I am enclosing a cheque for a hundred rupees and if you want more let me know. Have just paid your mess bills for March and April…' It seems likely that during 1932, Rabbit's marriage went wrong. Jai wrote:

> You are a silly little fool. Why do you think I am angry with you? My reason for not being able to write to you lately was that we are so busy playing polo.
>
> I am going to Jaipur for a couple of days on the 26th and will talk to Achrol (the thakur of Achrol) about your marriage. Don't worry I will fix you up with somebody really nice …

And later he confirmed:

> My Dear Rabbit,
>
> There is quite hopeful news about your marriage and I will fix you this summer with some nice girl. They want all sorts of guarantees, which I am accepting on your behalf, so don't let me down. I have sent for your horoscope…
>
> Yours
> Jai

In 1936, Rabbit remarried. Rabbit's new wife, Bunty, was a girl of great beauty and came from a simple family. She was quite unaccustomed to the ways of the court, but was often able to stand up to Jai. Once, she refused go to a place to which she was invited. Her ire was targeted at Jai. She felt that Jai did not assert himself strongly to discourage Rabbit from his waywardness. Jai managed to charm her back by going to see her personally and requesting her to come to a party, promising to 'put out a red carpet' for her. She relented and, when she arrived at the party, she was taken to an entrance different from the one used by all the other guests, one at which Jai literally had a red carpet laid. Laxman Singh Barwara, Rabbit's son, still treasures the photograph in his personal album.

The letters to Rabbit go on for many years, mainly dealing with Rabbit's recurring problems. In July 1936, Jai wrote:

> So glad you have realized now who are your well wishers and otherwise. My advice is to be friendly with all of them but trust none of them...

Jai was always extremely generous to his younger friend. In 1940, he wrote sending, not one hundred, but two thousand rupees.

In Jaipur, sycophants surrounded Jai. Even today, when the power of the maharajas has been abolished for nearly 45 years and their titles removed for almost 30 years, respect for royalty is deeply ingrained among people in the former princely states. It was hard for the young maharaja to know whom he could rely on as a friend. The advice that he gave Rabbit 'to be friendly to everyone but to trust no one', came from the experience Jai had gathered in the past 15 years.

In military parlance, it is said that a commander has to learn to be lonely. In those days, a maharaja was in a somewhat similar state. Everyone looked up to him with deference. However, occupying a lofty throne can become lonesome. Jai used to crave for informality from everyone, including his staff when not on duty. He used to tell his ADCs, 'When you are off duty, for God's sake don't call me Highness or I will go mad. Who can I talk to?' Major Sumer Singh of Nayla who was his constant companion for tennis and squash, reminisces that Jai insisted that he be treated like any other member at the Jaipur Club.

Jai had had a happy childhood till the age of 10, when he was pitchforked from Kota to City Palace at Jaipur. One can understand the psychological blow he suffered at that tender age. Whether it was because of this separation or in spite of it, Jai's attachment with his Isarda family was to last all his life. Jai had three sisters and one brother. His eldest sister, Gopal Kanwar, was married to the Maharaja of Panna. The second sister, Sajan Kanwar, got married to Maharaja Ajit Singh of Jodhpur. His elder brother, Bahadur Singh, subsequently succeeded at Isarda. Bahadur accompanied Jai during his early days, from Ram Bagh School to Mayo and Woolwich. Jai was next, but between him and Bahadur, one sibling died at the age of six months, allegedly due to an overdose of opium. After Jai, came a girl who also died an infant. Consequently, Chand Baisa, the youngest was the apple of everyone's eye.

Jai's entire Isarda family used to visit Jaipur during the Dussera festival and stay for a month. Sawai Singh, his father, being an extremely orthodox man, did not send Sajan Kanwar to Jaipur, since grown-up unmarried girls are not permitted to leave their homes. Consequently, she visited Jaipur only after her marriage. Chand was too young to be hobbled by this custom. She practically grew up in the royal environs.

Both First Her Highness and Second Her Highness greatly respected Jai's Isarda parents. When Second Her Highness wanted to have a hair cut, a hair stylist was called from Delhi. However, Jai warned Second Her Highness that Chand would go and tell Aapjisa (his Isarda father, Sawai Singh). On Jai's suggestion, Chand was given a hair cut first. So much was the awe in which Sawai Singh was held.

Jai would also go out of his way to look after his Jaipur mother, Maji Sahiba Tanwar, the youngest queen of Madho Singh, who was still living in City Palace. He asked First Her Highness to persuade Ma Sahiba to come to Ram Bagh at least once a week to spend the day, away from the claustrophobic environs of City Palace. He would punctiliously enquire about her welfare.

Second Her Highness was going to England a second time for the Queen's coronation in 1937.[5] Around this time, Chand fell ill. Doctors suggested that she be taken to Europe for medical treatment. Realizing that Aapjisa would never give his consent for such a trip, as also the fact that a visit abroad was absolutely imperative, Second Her Highness had Chand's passport prepared quietly and took her to London with her. She then requested Rao Chandrapal Singh to take her to Switzerland for the treatment. Tota Ramji, the advocate of Isarda family, learnt of this and informed Sawai Singh, who wrote detailed letters to Jai and Second Her Highness, censoring them for taking an unmarried girl abroad. A third letter was written to Chand herself, disowning her as his daughter. Second Her Highness reacted with equanimity saying that she would rather have Chand alive at the cost of tradition than have her sacrificed unattended at the altar of orthodoxy. This incident illustrates the kind of bigotry that Jai had to live with. His amplitude of experience extended from extreme ignorance to threatening to emulate a future king of England forsaking his throne for the sake of the woman he loved.[6]

Despite Sawai Singh's whims, his word was law as far Jai's family was concerned. Once, while he (as a thakur of Isarda) was going to City Palace to pay his regards to his own son Jai (as ruler of Jaipur), a car crossed him at the gate. On inquiring he learnt that First Her Highness was going to Khasa Kothi for her evening walk. Sawai Singh was annoyed that First Her Highness should travel in a car without proper purdah (curtains on the windows and rear). When Jai was told, he pointed out to his father that the glasses on the window were special. He, in fact, sat in the car to demonstrate to his father that no one could see the occupants of the car. However, Sawai Singh was not satisfied. The news of this incident reached First Her Highness.

She never again used a car without purdah.

---

1   The famous temple constructed by Ma Sahiba Tanwar still stands opposite the Reserve Police Lines near Chand Pol Gate. It is said that after Madho Singh II's death, when the rooms of Roop Rai were being searched for the first time, she threw a bundle full of jewels and currency across the wall. It landed in the courtyard of Ma Tanwar, who utilized the contents for the construction of this temple.

2   Eldest queen.

3   Author of *The Last Maharaja*.

4   Bill Clinton, former US president, visited this tiger reserve with his daughter Chelsea.

5   The first time she went abroad was for Joey's birth on the insistence of Ranjit Singh (of Jamnagar), who was her maternal uncle.

6   Jai had threatened that he would follow Edward's footsteps when opposition to his marriage to Gayatri Devi of Cooch Behar was becoming strident.

AS MAHARAJA

At the beginning of his reign, Jai spent little time over the affairs of the state, since ministers were in charge. Jai would ordinarily not interfere with the routine functioning of the administration. He appointed capable persons and left them to do the job. There were four aspirants for the prime minister's job. Mr Alexander, an Englishman and revenue member of the council; Amar Nath Atal, a Kashmiri (later the finance minister who handled all of Jai's private finances); the thakur of Chomu, who was by now out of the woods (after having opposed Jai's adoption); and Bhairon Singh Tanwar, who was in charge of hunts. Jai kept receiving conflicting reports about these people. He had learnt early that a king must be above intrigues and manipulation. He verified information from both sides. Consequently, he did not appoint any native prime minister till 1940.

Hunting was an important event in those days. The kings used to have their private hunting grounds and no-one could hunt in this area without the king's permission. Usually, visiting rajas from neighbouring principalities, or the king's guests were permitted to hunt in the royal reserves.

Sawai Ram Singh II had prohibited the shooting of the sambhar, deer, and tigers, except in the Sikar and Khetri *thikanas* of Shekhawati. Such restrictions were not applicable to the royal family. The game in those days was deer and wild boar.

Marudhar Kanwar, First Her Highness, gave birth to a daughter, Prem Kumari (Mickey) at Shimla in 1929, while Chand was at Jaipur and Jai at Woolwich. Jai returned to Jaipur and spoke to his wife at Shimla over the phone. He then teased Chand that First Her Highness would no longer love her. Chand was in tears, but First Her Highness spoke to her too and consoled her saying, 'I'll get a small doll for you to play with.'

The present His Highness Bhawani Singh was born in October 1931 at Jaipur. Bhawani Singh was the first male heir born to the Maharaja of Jaipur since Ram Singh II. There were, therefore, celebrations on a grand scale. According to Rajmata Gayatri Devi, he was nicknamed Bubbles by his English nurse because much champagne flowed on the day he was born. Bhawani Singh later grew up and joined the army.

Jai's visits to Europe used to be primarily polo oriented. He would play polo at least four times a week. There were three polo clubs in London—Roehampton, Hulingham, and Ranelagh, availing of the 10 polo grounds in London that were very active. Jai's passion for polo excluded even horse racing events, which he would occasionally attend only in a social capacity. However, while the visits to England provided Jai with a break from the tedium of being a maharaja, he got great ideas for the improvement and modernization of the administration, welfare of his subjects, as also reorganization of the army. This was also the occasion to make purchases.

Jai's tastes were impeccable. On his return, the number of English dishes in the kitchen would grow.

On returning, he would soon get down to the business of the state. Jai's upbringing, English education, prolonged stays abroad and an inclination for the West greatly influenced Jai's personality. Even if he spoke to his officers and the nobility in English, he was glad to hear them answer in the local dialect. It was in these days that Jai developed his strength as a king and matured fully. General Amar Singh was exuberant about the superb training received by Jai, as also his popularity. He noted that Jai mixed around with everyone easily, but kept people at a distance. Nobody could take liberties with him. His upbringing and frequent trips abroad gave him an advantage. It kept him away from the palace intrigues which was a part of court life in those days.

Even while he was trying to inject fresh ideas into his state from Europe, including the abolition of purdah by the ladies, he usually encountered unspoken resistance. He found it exasperating that his command, even over his own ADCs, was not total. It was more out of old world lethargy than deliberate disobedience. Some of the undated notes regarding his talks to the ADCs reflect his unenviable state of mind. One such note goes thus:

> Gentlemen, it is no pleasure for me to talk to you today as this is a repetition of the same things for the 100th time if not more… You have made failures of your career and today you exist because of my kindness, the softness of my heart, but you, instead of having any gratitude do nothing but take advantage for your own selfish purposes. This is my final talk with you all…before concluding… I would like to ask a favour of the ADCs that in future if any of them neglect their duty or make a blunder I hope they'll have the decency to put in their resignation on their own without being asked by me.

Jai's anger with his staff could be well understood. One particular incident had a rather strange result. In an effort to do away with the purdah system, he had once persuaded the ladies, against convention and their inclination, to come to the card room in Ram Bagh Palace. Fearing that male presence would act as a damper in the proceedings, he directed that none of the male staff would go near the card room. To his utter astonishment, he found a group of them gossiping right next to the forbidden room. Not only did he ban them from entering Ram Bagh Palace for a month but he also forfeited the silver jubilee medal that was due soon to one of them (he gave it to Rabbit instead).

His tussle with the staff continued because Jai was obsessed with details of protocol. This invariably led to slips, confusion, and exasperation. For instance, he would have his durbar seated two to three hours before any ceremony and yet claim credit for the waiting period having been halved as compared to the time of Madho Singh II.

Although Jai received a liberal education, he was a religious man. It was under the influence of Thakur Bahadur Singh (brother-in-law of Maharaja Ram Singh) that Jai developed an abiding and deep-rooted respect for religion and he participated in ceremonies punctiliously. The maharaja was traditionally a defender of the faith and Jai would perform his duties in this sphere to the hilt, including sacrificing a goat with his own hands in the temple of Shila Devi in Amber. Man Singh I from Jessore had brought the idol of Shila Devi and a temple was built there in 1604. Jai commissioned the doors of this temple to be made of silver as thanksgiving after he survived an air crash in 1939. The temple of Shila Devi is housed in the Amber Fort and though the fort now belongs to the state, the temple remains part of the private property of the Maharaja of Jaipur. The other temple of importance was the Govind Dev Temple built in 1735, whose deity had been brought from Vrindavan by Sawai Jai Singh. All the Kachhwaha rulers ruled over the subjects of Jaipur in the name of Govind Dev. A third temple of Jamwa Mata, 30 kms off Jaipur and located at Ramgarh, is the oldest. It was built in 1007 after the Kachhwahas first conquered the Meenas and began ruling Amber.

Traditionally, the king would visit the temple of Shila Devi at Amber before leaving the state, as well as immediately on his return. Jai was very particular about these religious duties. He would perform the most complicated rituals to the last detail. He even observed the fast for Kali Mata. His religious inclination was almost as inscrutable as that of Madho Singh II. He used to pray every day, including during his sojourns in England. He would also always pray before a polo match. Like Madho Singh II, he also carried the idol of Govind Dev with him whenever he went abroad (during World War II he carried the photo of Durga, the Goddess of War). However, although Jai was religious, he was not superstitious.

Tales of Jai's parsimony are legion. It is possible that he may have inherited this habit from his tight-fisted father (of Isarda). His close friends indulgently called it 'a great respect for cash', which translated into his never carrying it on his person. Jai was once holidaying in the south of France with another maharaja. They used to go out often. Whenever it was time to reach for the wallet, Jai invariably asked the other maharaja's ADC to settle the bill because he had forgotten to get his purse. In early 1932, he was made the Patron of the Old Boys Association of Mayo College. Even on this occasion, he refused to give Rs 1000 as contribution, ostensibly because he could not afford it. He wanted the frugality to be followed by his family as well. It occasioned an interesting incident. The story goes that Bhawani Singh was once censured by Jai for his extravagance. Jai narrated to him stories about his own frugal habits. Bubbles responded, tongue in cheek, by saying that he was the son of His Highness Jaipur whereas Jai was the son of the thakur of Isarda.

Jai had once hired some instructors to train the Sawai Man Guards, promising them a packet of 20 pounds per month. When they arrived, Jai wanted to reduce their salary to 15 pounds. On another occasion, Amar Singh records the fuss Jai created about a fountain pen being bought out of regimental funds. And yet another time, there was a commotion as to who would pay the monthly salary of Rs 25 per month to the servant who was supposed to look after a cow. The cow had been presented to the Maharaja of Kishangarh. However, despite his stinginess, Jai never invoked any bitter or hard feelings. Such was his charm.

In 1934, Jai had already been made an honorary captain in the Indian Army. Later, when he had little to do in England except play polo, he became attached to the Life Guards in 1937. He was popular there. Jai's exalted status of being the maharaja or his commission in a British regiment did not prevent him from indulging in pranks. He would usually race around Hyde Park in his famous Bentley with policemen chasing him. Before they could catch up, he would get into the barracks and claim diplomatic immunity. This high-spirited behaviour was typical whenever he went. Once, when flying himself back from Calcutta with his ADC, he landed at Allahabad to find the canteen closed. Jai was hungry, so he asked the aides to break it open to get some food. When the police arrived, he asked them to send the bill for the damages.

Although, Jai considered his attachment with the Life Guards a matter of great honour, he was rather insouciant about it. He would start fencing in Lord Roderick's office. Having slashed a painting once, he switched over to using an umbrella instead. At that time, he was staying in Dorchester Hotel and whenever he came to Lord Roderick's room he would be offered black coffee or brandy and ginger ale depending on the menu of the previous evening. A few weeks after joining the Life Guards, he and Lord Roderick were transferred to Combermere Barracks at Windsor. Here, they went through a war exercise under the keen eye of a British general. They were to move from one place to another under camouflage, undetected by the enemy. Both of them galloped across in their anxiety to win. The general was furious. Later, when Jai was introduced to the general as the Maharaja of Jaipur, the waiting general asked Jai whether he should salute him. Instead, Jai hastily saluted the general!

Planning to undo the damage, they bribed their way through in the next exercise. They were supposed to ambush the enemy whose approach was not known. A needy postman, appropriately bribed, obliged them with the correct information. They reached the right spot for ambush. An impressed general asked how they discerned the enemy intentions so accurately. He was told the truth.

Jai was susceptible to accidents because of his boisterous and spirited behaviour. The first one occurred during a polo match in December 1936 in Jaipur, when he and Gerald Balding collided head on. Jai suffered severe injuries due to which he was sent to Austria for treatment in January 1937. He was kept on traction. His ADC Maj. Parbat Singh was a worried man. When the aide's anxiety was conveyed to Jai, he brushed aside the concern and asked the aide to be more useful by replacing the fat nurse attending to him by a shapely one. A little improved, Jai shifted to Hotel Bristol for further treatment. At that time Virginia (Cherill) who married Cary Grant and later the Earl of Gersey, was staying at Ram Bagh Palace. She visited Jai in Vienna to bolster his spirits.

The deposed Maharaja of Alwar (a state near Jaipur), with his three dozen concubines, also came to look up Jai and occupied one whole floor in Hotel Bristol in Austria. Alwar was an amoral person and an intransigent character, who once burnt his favourite polo pony after losing a match by pouring kerosene on the pony and setting her aflame in full public glare. Alwar was a bizarre combination of eccentricity, malice, and ego gone awry due to almost unbridled power. Stories about his obnoxious behaviour are legion. While holidaying at Mount Abu once, Bikaner inadvertently or otherwise omitted to invite Alwar for a large party. Alwar sent out his men to buy all the food available within a radius of 40 miles. Bikaner was forced to cancel his party. He invited Alwar the next time. Such outrageous behaviour was not peculiar to Alwar alone. There were other maharajas who had a reputation for eccentricity and depravity. The Nawab of Junagarh squandered a fortune on the wedding of his favourite dog. The Maharaja of Alwar, snubbed by a salesman in London, purchased all the Rolls-Royces available in the showroom and used them as garbage trucks in his state. The Nizam of Hyderabad used diamonds the size of eggs as paperweights. Maharaja Ummaid Singh of Jodhpur was in London with his wife during the polo season in the early twenties. His Maharani, being in purdah, was a natural target for the society tabloids. The Queen of England, in fact, enquired whether the king could have a look at her. The query was ignored. One enterprising photographer snapped the ankles of Her

Highness Jodhpur while alighting from a car. The photograph was published in a newspaper. With alacrity the Jodhpur party went out and purchased every single paper before they could be dispatched to India.

Alwar, in fact, was on the verge of being deposed many times. Every time such an occasion arose, he would manage to dine with the Secretary of State for India in London. The British tolerated his pederasty without censor. As Quentin Crewe writes:

> Alwar's method of protest against British domination was to adopt an excessively Hindu posture. He affected to believe that he was a reincarnation of Rama. He would not allow any leather in his palaces and his Rolls-Royces were upholstered in French needlepoint. He would refuse to shake hands with any European unless she was wearing gloves. At one point, when he was in danger of deposition, he was invited to Buckingham Palace. His advisors besought him to take off his gloves when he met King George V. He promised to do so. Before shaking hands, he drew off his gloves with great ostentation. He had on another pair underneath.

Such were the times of the high and mighty. On the other hand, Jhilai, who had almost become a king, felt he was getting a raw deal. Once, when plague broke out in the state, Jhilai had all his subjects inoculated at a personal expense of Rs 3000. Since Jhilai had no heir, he wanted to adopt his own brother. Jai refused permission. Jhilai's brother, however, could not have succeeded him in any event, as he was murdered in 1937. Subsequently, Jai asked Jhilai to adopt his (Jai's) son. Thus, Jhilai adopted Maharaja Jai Singh (Joey), Jai's elder son from Second Her Highness.

THE MOST BEAUTIFUL WOMAN

In England, Jai became acquainted with the widow of the Maharaja of Cooch Behar (earlier Princess Indira Gaekwar of Baroda) known to everyone as Ma. She was the daughter of the Maharaja of Baroda. She had broken off her betrothal to the Maharaja of Gwalior in 1912 in favour of the younger brother of the Maharaja of Cooch Behar. Despite fierce opposition from her parents, she married him in 1913 in London. Her parents did not attend the marriage.[1] Her husband's elder brother (the Maharaja of Cooch Behar, Raj Rajendra Narayan) had fallen in love with an English actress, Edna May. He, too, was denied permission to marry. He drank himself to death in 1913. The younger brother succeeded him. Unfortunately, he also died at the age of 36, leaving behind a widow (Ma), all of 30 years of age, with five children. However, Ma was made of sterner stuff. She educated her children and took them to England for schooling. She herself became an active member of society in London.

The rapport that built up between Jai and Ma in London lasted lifelong. It was an important, almost indispensable, aspect of Jai's life later.

After their introduction in London, Ma used to visit Jaipur frequently. Similarly, when Jai used to be in Calcutta playing polo, he would stay at the Cooch Behar mansion, Woodlands.

Jai's third wife, Gayatri Devi, was her daughter.

Gayatri Devi (maiden name Ayesha) and Jai first met at Calcutta. After graduating from Woolwich, Jai reached Calcutta for polo during the Christmas holidays of 1931. Gayatri was then 12 and Jai nearly 21. The venue was Woodlands, the house of the royal family of Cooch Behar in Calcutta. Gayatri was pre-disposed towards Jai, having read his description by Rosita Forbes, an English writer, in *India of the Princes*:

> Because of his appearance and his charm, his possessions and his feats on horseback, this exceedingly good-looking young man, famous as a sportsman in three continents, occupies in the imagination of the Indian general public much the same position as the Princes of Wales did in the minds of working men (in England). In no other way can I suggest the universal popularity combined with a rather breathless wonder, as to what he will do next, which surrounds this best known of India's young rulers.

That was enough to excite Gayatri's imagination and she gladly gave up her room for Jai, a sacrifice she would hardly have acceded to, for any lesser mortal. Whenever he got time off from polo, he used to play tennis with Gayatri and Maneka (Gayatri's elder sister). Chivalrous as Jai was, he would call in an ADC to make a foursome and let the young girls carry the game.[2] For the first year, it was only a few tennis matches and an odd cycle race with Gayatri. Gayatri addressed Jai as Your Highness, since in her own words, Jai was 'quite outside my orbit'.

The next year, Jai returned to Calcutta for the polo season.

During one of the post-victory celebrations, a euphoric Ma offered Jai 'anything you want'. He asked for Gayatri to join him for the celebration dinner at Firpo's, one of the most fashionable restaurants in Calcutta. Gayatri was a mere 13. A proper dress and footwear had to be acquired for her. Gayatri still remembers the hours she and her maid spent in looking for the footwear that would match the dress. During dinner, Jai helped her cut up the partridge, an art to which Gayatri was yet unaccustomed. The tender loving care had begun. The chauffeur drove her back home, 'still dizzy and unbelieving'.

Their next rendezvous was to take place soon, in Woodlands itself. Jai developed a knee ailment and was confined to bed. He invited Gayatri and Maneka for supper one night, when the rest of the inmates were dining out. The evening is best described in Gayatri's own words:

> We were having a lively time, when promptly at 9 o'clock, our governess came to take us off to bed. I suppose Jai must have seen our disappointment because he persuaded her to let us stay a little longer by telling her, quite untruthfully, that Ma had given permission to stay up late. He rose still further in our estimation when he threw a piece of toast at her departing back and then offered us champagne from his glass to celebrate the success of the Jaipur team. I said primly that I never drank out of some one else's glass and, to Maneka's suppressed fury, was given a full glass of my own. After that, I began to have more ambitious daydreams—that the floor of his room which was immediately above the one that Maneka and I shared would fall through in the middle of the night, landing him (miraculously uninjured) in our room to spent the rest of the night with us. I even began wishing for something that seemed to me even more unlikely—that I would grow up to be beautiful and that Jai would actually kiss me.

Jai's second wedding to Kishore Kanwar in 1932 took place around this time.

When Gayatri shot her first panther, the news travelled through Ma to Jai, who promptly cabled congratulations.[3] This was in 1932, when Jai had returned after a successful polo season in England. Ma decided to visit Inderjeet, Gayatri's brother, who was studying at Mayo College, on her way to Baroda. Since Ajmer and Jaipur lie in close proximity, Jai invited the whole family to visit Jaipur. Not surprisingly, Jai received them at the station himself, with all his paraphernalia. This was Gayatri's first visit to Jaipur, which she called the 'prettiest (place) she had ever seen'. The guests were lodged at Ram Bagh Palace. Jai personally escorted them to the old capital, Amber, where, in course of the conversations, he narrated his entire family history to Gayatri.

The next day, a splendid party was organized for the guests. Gayatri was enjoying herself with the other girls, when Jai entered the room for a few minutes and then left soon thereafter. Gayatri remembers that 'although it was a charming and beautifully organized party, the pleasure dimmed for me as soon as he departed.' The next day, Jai took Gayatri out for a ride. During the ride, Jai made some suggestions to Gayatri and several times corrected the position of her hands and riding posture. His advice went unheeded. When Jai complained to Ma, Gayatri's reply to her mother was: 'I will do what he tells me, but not in his presence.' Gayatri confesses that although she was only 14, she was head over heels in love with Jai.

It was after this visit that Jai told Ma that he wanted to marry Gayatri when she grew up. Ma scoffed at the idea, saying she had never heard 'such sentimental rubbish'. It was exactly six years later that they got married.

Jai's annual visits to Calcutta every winter for the polo season continued, and Jai always treated Gayatri as a 'specially nice friend'. Subsequently, Gayatri was sent to Shanti Niketan, which was run by Noble Laureate Rabindranath Tagore. Indira Gandhi had just graduated from Shanti Niketan around this time. Thereafter, Gayatri was sent to Switzerland to finish her schooling.

Keeping in step with history, Gayatri's elder sister Ila had secretly married Romendra Kishore Dev Varma, the cousin of the Maharaja of Tripura. It was a registered marriage, which was kept a secret. When Gayatri moved to London with the entire family for further studies, Jai was also in London. Ma took Ila back to Cooch Behar for a proper Hindu wedding, leaving Maneka and Gayatri in London in the care of her mother (Gayatri's grandmother) and a baroness. During this period, Jai tried to take Gayatri and Maneka out but Gayatri's grandmother refused permission. Subsequently, Jai persuaded Hanut Singh of Jodhpur to invite Gayatri and Maneka for a polo match. Gayatri's grandmother permitted them to accept the invitation. As was bound to happen, Jai and Gayatri went out to watch the match alone.

Gayatri was 16 when Jai formally proposed to her. For good measure, he added: 'Before I ask Ma and go through all the proper formalities, I would like to know what you feel. Remember I play polo and ride and fly and I may have a horrible accident; still will you marry me?' To Gayatri's prompt 'Yes', Jai said, 'Don't answer immediately. Think about it for a moment. You still have to finish school. There is plenty of time. You don't have to say "yes" if you don't mean it.' Gayatri insisted that she wanted to marry him. Jai then asked her to write to Ma and tell her. Jai planned to speak to Ma later.

Thereafter, both of them met almost everyday, hoodwinking the grandmother. They would generally meet at Berkeley Hotel. The secret meeting was too conspicuous an event (Jai could not have been inconspicuous) and the entire hotel staff knew that a sizzling affair was on.

This happy interlude came at a time when Jai was in London for polo and Gayatri was waiting to join her Swiss School in September. She had four months at her disposal, so was made to join a school, Monkey Club.

Their meetings continued though Jai was extremely busy in London, leading a hectic social life and playing polo. Yet, they would manage a quick snack at the Berkeley Buttery almost every day. They would walk like strangers to the car and would speak only once they were inside the car. They were getting close. In Gayatri's own words: 'By now, I was less shy of Jai, though still a little in awe of him, but we laughed a lot, I remember, and had our private jokes, and then being in love takes up an awful lot of conversation. One talks endlessly about oneself and listens enthralled to the tiniest details about the other person's life or opinions.'

Later, whenever Gayatri went to Berkeley Hotel alone, the *maître d'hôtel* would come and whisper to Gayatri, 'It is not the same without His Highness, is it?' Those were the days when Maneka and Gayatri were living under the watchful eye of their grandmother and the baroness. Even the telephones were monitored, so Gayatri had to go to the telephone booth in Pont Street from where the rendezvous for the evening would be fixed. Jai would arrive in his Bentley and park at Wilton Crescent. Gayatri would concoct a story about going out to the cinema with her girlfriends. She would go dressed casually, get into the car, and then the lovebirds would drive away. Once, in a careless moment, Jai dropped her off right in front of the house. It was then that Maneka learnt of Gayatri's escapades. Subsequently, Maneka, then Baby (the other sister), and Inderjeet, all joined in the conspiracy. At times, they would plan a movie together. Jai would pick up Gayatri from the cinema hall, and the others would go in to watch the movie. On the way back from the theatre, they would tell Gayatri the story.

Despite being courageous enough to hoodwink her grandmother and the baroness, Gayatri was very hesitant in writing to her mother about the proposal. After the holidays in Dinard, Gayatri went to Lausanne to join school. Of these heady days, Gayatri writes in her autobiography, A *Princess Remembers:*

> … looking back on it all now I see that those times were much more fun than an ordinary approved courtship would have been. There was the challenge of outwitting our elders, of arranging secret meetings, of working out how to have letters posted without the knowledge of the ADCs, the governess or clerks who usually handled this chore. And every now and again, there was the marvellous, unheard of liberty of going for a drive in the country with Jai, of a stolen dinner at Bray, or of an outing on the river in a boat. Altogether, it was a lovely and intoxicating time. We sealed it for ourselves by buying gold rings for each other with our names engraved inside. I had carefully hoarded my pocket money to be able to buy this.

Gayatri was jolted out of her reverie when she received a cable from Jai saying 'Cannot understand why you haven't written to Ma. What is wrong?' Apparently, Jai had spoken to Ma, who was blissfully unaware of the shenanigans. For once, Gayatri thought that Jai must have imagined she had changed her mind. She spoke to Dr Chandrachud, an old friend, and a man of immense maturity and patience. On his advice, she cabled Jai saying, 'You have misunderstood me. Am writing.'

Then she wrote a letter to him saying, 'I know I should have written to Ma earlier, but I did not have the courage and I did not know what to say. But, now I have done it, and I hope you are not annoyed with me. I didn't mean to make you think I didn't want to marry you, because I do.' Meanwhile, she had written to Ma: 'I think the Maharaja of Jaipur must have spoken to you. I hope you don't mind our arranging all this without asking you first. When His Highness asked me directly about marrying him, there was nothing I could do, so I agreed.' There were no further ripples and despite the minor hiccup, the flight was apparently on course.

After joining the school at Brillantmont, Gayatri wrote to Jai frequently. Jai had suffered a severe back injury during a polo match and was in Vienna for treatment. After his convalescence, he went to Lausanne to see Gayatri. Since the students could go out only with family members, Gayatri told the oldest lie in the lover's book—that Jai was her cousin. They spent a happy day together. The finale was a dinner at Palace Hotel and Jai nearly missed the train. Apparently, on some suspicion, all of Gayatri's letters were censored thereafter. This was the time when Edward VIII of England abdicated his throne for, as he said, 'the woman I love'. Heady days for Gayatri indeed. She understood every word Edward said and more importantly, every word that he did not say.

In the summers that followed, Jai was in London with Second Her Highness and his children. Royalty from all over India had congregated in London for the coronation of George VI. There was, therefore, little chance of Jai and Gayatri meeting alone.

Yet, Jai and Gayatri's affair became a part of the social gossip. Ma was very fond of Jai, but was still not comfortable about the prospect of their marriage, on more than one count.

Gayatri would be Jai's third wife. By marrying Jai, Gayatri could possibly hurt Second Her Highness Kishore Kanwar, who got along very well with Gayatri's entire family. There was also the apprehension that Gayatri might have to spend her entire life in purdah. Initially, Ma had ignored the affair as an infatuation and hoped that it would ebb. However, that was not to be. There was also the apprehension that Jai might marry for the fourth time. Ma, therefore, tried her best to keep Gayatri occupied in all kinds of activities, without directly prohibiting her interaction with Jai.

There was a brief interlude in Cannes, where Gayatri joined her mother after the school session. Jai was also present. Jai and Gayatri would go for a swim in the sea before Ma got up. For the evening round of social commitments, only Jai and Ma used to go out. Gayatri was still considered too young to join them on such occasions. It was in Cannes that she had her first quarrel with Jai. In her words,

> One day as Jai was going into the sea for a swim, he took off the ring I had given him in London and handed it to Maneka to hold for him. I was seized with a fit of jealousy because he had given it to her instead of to me and grabbed the ring from her and threw it into the sea. Jai took me by the shoulders and walked with me to the end of the pier, explaining very gently as we went that he hadn't meant to hurt my feelings. Just as I had calmed down, my ruffled feelings smoothed into place, he suddenly pushed me into the sea, fully dressed. I emerged furious and threw his shoes into the water in revenge. I arrived late for lunch, with my hair still wet, wearing shorts, and seething. Maneka, who was very prim at that stage, was most dismayed. But if I had hoped for any satisfactory matching fury from Jai, I was disappointed. His only comment, delivered with the most maddening cheerfulness, was that his shoes now fit him much better after their shrinking; they had been a size too large before. However, our quarrels were rare, and parting from Jai grew worse and worse. When he left Cannes I ran the length of the platform,

holding his hand as the train pulled out. He went on to Biarritz and telephoned me every day from there. His calls always came in the evening and, because we didn't want them to be monitored, I spent hours sitting on the floor of the telephone booth in the hotel lobby so that no one would see me waiting for the call to come through.

In June, Gayatri and her family toured Europe. War clouds were gathering. Conversations gravitated towards Hitler and the Nazis. Jai joined Gayatri and her family in Budapest. Naturally, Gayatri describes the beauty of Budapest in the most romantic language.

But in spite of the ominous news stories and the edgy atmosphere we felt at parties, a sense of time running out, I remember it as a golden and enchanted summer. This was because Jai joined us in Budapest. The city seemed at its most beautiful, with flowers everywhere and the evenings filled with the lovely sound, alternately plaintive and merry, of the zithers. There was a big tennis tournament, and we went to watch the matches. I still have pictures of them, Jai sitting by my side, both of us looking so young and happy. We went swimming. We went to see horses and horse shows, which we all loved. We drove into the country and stopped at inns or restaurants, gay with flowers, wild with gypsy music. We drank the local wines and took long walks in the long, melting European summer evenings. I remember being distressed only when the boys would ask the band to play, 'The Merry Widow Waltz', and then tell me as if it were a joke that there would soon be a war and they would all be killed and I would be the 'Merry Widow'. It all seems unremarkable as I describe it. I suppose it was so magical to me only because I was surrounded by all the people dearest to me and most of all because I was young, and in love, and Jai was with me constantly. Even through the rosy glow that my happiness spread on everything, it was difficult in the late summer of 1938 to ignore for long the menace of war and soon Ma felt it was time for us to return to London.

Ma returned to Baroda to attend to her ailing father. Maneka
and Gayatri later reached Bombay by ship. Jai was with Ma to
receive them at the port. Such was the place Gayatri occupied
in Jai's life when Jai had already been enjoying full sovereign
powers for seven years. That evening Jai and Gayatri went to
the Wellington Club which was popular among the elite of
society. It was a thrilling situation for the lovers when the
group sitting in the garden kept on getting larger with new
friends joining in, but Jai and Gayatri managed to sit next to
each other all the time.

Soon thereafter, Gayatri went back to Calcutta. Jai
followed and stayed at Woodlands. Every morning they used
to ride together. The social demands were heavy and by now
Gayatri was considered grown-up enough to join them
occasionally. The correspondence between Jai and Gayatri
indicates the passion of the relationship. He used to refer to
her by many names, but most often it was Pat.

The Palace, Jaipur
28 Nov 1937

My Beloved Pat,

You make me so happy darling I wish you could see me. It was
heaven talking to you. Only I wish you had not insisted on business,
rather I wanted to know more about you darling... What is the idea
of going to Agra and seeing the Taj? Beloved let's keep plans like
that, for us to do together, and if you only do it for motoring sake
please be more intelligent towards this side. You know how I long to
see you and be with you so please beloved use the brains (if any) in
the right direction!!

All my love (to) you
Forever Jai.

A lovelorn maharaja, despite his hectic schedule, found time to write to her frequently:

> Pat darling,
>
> I am feeling miserable and very unhappy as there is no news from you, but I suppose such is life. So drop me a line. If you can, as you know just one word from you makes all the difference to me. I need not tell you how I feel about you. Hardly a moment passes when you are not in my thoughts and I just long to see you again. I hope you are having fun in C.B. All my love darling,
>
> Yours always,
>
> Jai

Jai and Gayatri's love was the stuff of legends. Handsome, debonair Jai, with his infectious gaiety and gentle charm and graceful Gayatri, stunningly beautiful and ever elegant as his consort. They made headlines wherever they went. The ostensibly enchanting Jai developed an unusually strong streak in matters concerning Gayatri. He wanted her for his wife. He also knew that it was a Sisyphean task. But the perils of the problem never dampened his enthusiasm for the enterprise. The protean Jai negotiated his way through the labyrinth. But more of that later.

---

1   It may be interesting to note that Ma's father had been brought up in a village 200 miles south of Baroda. The Dowager Maharani of Baroda adopted him when the British deposed her own son for misrule.

2   Gayatri's mother (Ma) was a tennis player of some talent. She challenged Jai to a game of tennis. Her bravado was based on feedback from her daughters. Somehow, Jai temporarily forgot his chivalry. Ma lost hopelessly and was naturally furious with the girls.

3   Gayatri was overjoyed and called it '… almost as thrilling as the kill itself'.

THE SIKAR REBELLION

The Government of India Act came into being in 1935, under which a Federation Committee was set up. The act aimed to associate the Indian states with British India as equal partners in a loose federation. The destiny of India as a nation was being forged and the pattern on the skein had begun to surface. Despite long patronage by the British, a few relics of feudalism survived in Rajputana. In 1938, the Sikar rebellion took place, which was a typical example of the changing times. This incident was to alter Jai's life totally, though imperceptibly.

Shekha, one of the Kachhwahas of Amber, had captured Sikar and Jhunjhunu, popularly known as Shekhawati. Later, Shekha declared himself independent. Sawai Jai Singh (who established Jaipur) brought Shekhawati back into the fold, but after Jai Singh's death, Shekhawati played up again. Jaipur was almost helpless in taming Shekhawati till the treaty with the British was signed in 1818. The alliance ensured, among other things, that Shekhawati paid its tributes to Jaipur regularly. While the revenue source was ensured, a sense of alienation among the people of Shekhawati continued and the tribute was paid grudgingly. To Jai, this area was too insignificant to be noticed.

Maharaja Ram Singh II had laid down hunting rules banning the shikar of tigers, bears, and the sambhar. Rao Raja Kalyan Singh of Sikar and the Raja of Khetri were kept out of the ambit of this order. However, in 1933, when Rao Raja Kalyan Singh shot a tiger, Jai wanted to fine him Rs 500. Amar Singh interceded on behalf of Sikar. Although Jai acceded to Amar Singh, he insisted that Sikar accept an Englishman as a senior member of his council. Rao Raja Kalyan Singh had no option but to agree. Sikar, however, was a cunning man. He provided the Englishman with enough money to retire comfortably. He made life miserable for the second one. Captain A.W.T. Webb, the third member who joined his council in June 1934, dexterously avoided the Rao Raja's manipulations and started progressive reforms, gradually increasing the revenue of Sikar by Rs 1,00,000. The Rao Raja was annoyed, since the improvement in a way, reflected his incompetence. His protests were vociferous but in vain. There was considerable dissonance between Jaipur and Sikar and the latent exasperation in the public, waiting to manifest itself, received an unexpected and unsolicited ally in the Rao Raja.

The whole thing came to a head when C.N. Willis, a retired civil service officer, was asked to submit a report on the 'Land Tenures and special powers of Thikanedars in Jaipur State'. The report was a cornucopia of contradictions. However, it was considered useful for the Jaipur council which could use it to further rein in an intransigent Sikar. A Commission of Enquiry was appointed to probe the matters further. This angered Sikar, an unlettered man who never let his illiteracy interfere with his intransigency. He engaged a barrister from Lucknow to present the case of Sikar in a convincing manner. To the grave misfortune of Sikar, the author of the original report, Willis, was himself the chairman of the commission. The conclusions were not far to seek.

The culmination of Captain Webb's work, Wills's report and the protest of the unfortunate and harassed Rao Raja led to a very unusual finale. Sir Beauchamp St John, the prime minister of Jaipur, took away the powers of the Rao Raja for 10 years, merely permitting him to stay at Sikar, with a privy purse of Rs 1,00,000. The education of his son was to be handled by the (English) council member. The confiscation of these powers had the added advantage of permitting the renewal of Webb's contract at Sikar, which was to expire soon.

A revolt in Sikar—a perfect example of Alexander Pope's observation in *The Rape of the Lock* – 'what mighty contests rise from trivial things'—erupted. The revolt broke out when the Rao Raja saw his son Hardayal do hard physical training one day. Hardayal, the apple of his father's eye, was born in 1921. He was betrothed to the daughter of the Maharaja of Dharangadhra (Gujarat) before he entered his teens. The marriage was to take place in 1938. Hardayal was initially sent to Mayo but was later withdrawn. On the question of his further education, Jai decided that he should go to Cambridge. There was strong opposition all round to this suggestion, as education in England would mean postponement of the marriage. Sir Beauchamp, the prime minister, also did not like the idea of sending the prince abroad for education against the desire of all and sundry. It was considered an unsolicited interference in a purely private matter. The Rao Raja was opposed to any move that would take his son so far away from him. Besides, being uneducated himself, he could hardly appreciate the need for Western education for his son. However, the most painful aspect was that he had not been consulted on the matter even once. Jai, being against an early marriage, overruled the protest and Sikar was told that his son would indeed go abroad for further studies. Sikar appealed to Delhi. Delhi remanded him back to Jaipur. An anguished Rao Raja wrote letters to the First and Second Her Highnesses of Jaipur, as well as to the wife of the prime minister of Jaipur. Finding no support, Sikar retreated, sulking, into his shell. But the resentment was too conspicuous to be ignored.

To settle matters, Jai sent for Rao Raja Sikar, who refused to come. Jai sent Webb, F.S. Young, the overzealous police chief of Jaipur, and a couple of nobles to persuade the Rao Raja to come to the city. When this party reached Sikar, they found that the Rao Raja was staying outside the city in a rest house with an unusually large congregation of Rajputs. When they requested the Rao Raja to accompany them, he abruptly got up saying that he had to attend to his ailing wife. Young put his hand on the Rao Raja's shoulder to beseech him to come. This gesture was taken by the locals to mean that the Rao Raja had been arrested. The crowd went out of control, knocked Young aside and carried the Rao Raja to the fort on their shoulders, closing the gates behind them and declaring a strike. Young asked for reinforcements from Jaipur. However, the Jaipur Council refused to send a police contingent and decided to send another deputation under Amar Singh.

Amar Singh went laden with promises to speak to Sikar regarding his son. These promises were: (a) his son would go to England for his education with Jai in a ship, and not by air; (b) he would return with Jai within four months; (c) the date of the marriage would be decided by Jaipur and Dharangadhra mutually; (d) the Rao Raja would be permitted to go to Jaipur when the tensions ebbed; and (e) the Rao Raja could go to England to see his son if he so desired at a later date, the expenses of the trip being borne by Jaipur.

Amar Singh reached Sikar to find a swelling crowd of Rajputs in and around the fort. The Rao Raja welcomed Amar Singh, since they were old friends. After unburdening himself concerning the injustice meted out to him, the Rao Raja agreed to accompany Amar Singh. The next day when they were about to leave, the Rajput throng tried to extract promises from Amar Singh that were quite beyond his brief. Thus, although the Rao Raja was willing to go to Jaipur, Amar Singh was helpless and had to return alone. Amar Singh had a towering stature and the failure of his mission should have jolted Jai out of his reverie. But more was to follow. The situation was becoming at once tense and comic. The discomfiture of Jaipur in this scenario was thoroughly relished by two organizations, the Jat Maha Sabha and the Praja Mandal of Jaipur.

Today the Jats are a class of cultivators spread all over Rajasthan. In those days, the Jats ruled Bharatpur and Dholpur. Jaipur, Jhunjhunu, and Sikar were (and still are) dominated by Jats and till date they outnumber any single caste by far. Several minor incidents added fuel to the fire. Jat bridegrooms were not permitted to ride horses in those days. When a Jat bridegroom rode a horse past a Rajput house, it created an ugly scene. There was a fraeas and the incident snowballed into a disaster, leading to police firing in which a few Jats died and many more were arrested. The Jats were then forbidden from entering Jaipur State; they were also not permitted to carry weapons. Other measures were also initiated to keep them under control.

— The Shekhawati Jats had always felt discriminated against. The recent events added to their resentment. They refused to pay rent in 1933 in Sikar. There were public demonstrations, which continued for the next two years. Police help had to be sought from Jaipur, and a settlement was arrived at by permitting Jats to enter government service. The Jats formed the Jat Kisan Sabha in 1935 to put up an organized fight. Even though things were gradually looking up for the Jats, the bitter taste of past repression had not faded, when the Sikar rebellion erupted.

The second organization, watching from the sidelines with glee, was the Praja Mandal of Jaipur. This organization included intellectuals and educated urban youth who were intimately associated with the Indian National Congress. Ironically, the Praja Mandal was formed in 1931, the same year in which Jai assumed full powers as a maharaja. Jamna Lal Bajaj was their leader in Rajputana.

The Praja Mandal and the Jaipur Government always enjoyed cordial relations. In 1938, at the first annual session of Praja Mandal, the chairman of the reception committee said:

> We would preserve the Crown with all its magnificent glory, with all its historic association, with all its rights and privileges and with all our traditional loyalty. The elimination of the monarchy or causing any disaffection or disloyalty to the person and throne of His Highness does not and can never appeal to us.

Heera Lal Shastri acknowledged the relationship in his letter to Police Chief Freddie Young in 1939:

> The position, as between the Government and the Mandal in Jaipur, is unique... Jaipur's name will go down in history for the world will see in due course of time that there were officials and public workers in Jaipur who achieved the same object with mutual

agreement, which elsewhere was almost invariably achieved after agony and heartburn on both sides.

The Praja Mandal sought representative government and, in a way, they even supported the small thakurs, since they were as much discriminated against by the royalty as the ordinary people were. However, in Sikar even the smaller thakurs rallied around the Rao Raja, leading to Bajaj withdrawing from the scene, after initially offering his good offices.

This was the situation on 21 April, when the prime minister of Jaipur, Sir Beauchamp, decided to make another attempt himself. Amar Singh accompanied him. The prime minister met two deputations. The first one was of the Rao Raja and his big thakurs and the second one was of the Jats, the Praja Mandal, and the lesser mortals of those days. The Rao Raja had convinced the Praja Mandal that he would provide a representative government after the Sikar episode. The result was that both the delegations wanted the Rao Raja to be restored for their own (albeit different) purposes. They were primarily aiming at throwing off the yoke of Jaipur. At that time Arthur Lothian was the agent to the governor general. He played an admirable part and tactfully managed to take the Rao Raja out of Sikar to Jaipur.

In the parleys that followed, Jai was forced to abandon his intention of sending the Rao Raja's son to England for education. He also granted amnesty to the followers of the Rao Raja who were involved in the fiasco. The Rao Raja presented his *nazar* to Jai and asked for his forgiveness. Having settled everything, Jai sailed to England on 7 May as planned.

A Commission of Enquiry was appointed to investigate the entire episode. However, the day after Jai left, the prime minister passed an order taking the administration of Sikar under the Court of Wards. Ostensibly, the Rao Raja was unable to govern his *thikana,* owing to mental infirmity. The prime minister ordered troops to enter Sikar. Such insensitivity re-ignited the fire. Public disenchantment flared up and the strike in Sikar resumed.

A Commission of Enquiry was finally set up. The Jats and the Praja Mandal continued fishing in troubled waters at Sikar, taking care of their interests. There was another unfortunate incident in which 70 belligerent and armed Rajputs arrived in Sikar by train. The overzealous police chief, Young, ordered them back. The inept handling of the situation made matters worse. The Rajputs fired at the police, killing one policeman. Reprisals were sharp and swift. The situation was promptly brought under control, but the whole episode made headlines. It drew the attention of the House of Commons. An unhappy Jai had to return from his England sojourn on 16 July, a month earlier than scheduled. Lothian persuaded him to go to Sikar himself. So, finally, Jai's did go to Sikar.

The aura of royalty was sufficient for the thaw. All demands were withdrawn and the entire episode vanished in a whiff of smoke. However, it left an indelible mark on Jai psyche.

Jai's thinking changed dramatically. So far the administration had been in the hands of the British aristocracy. Taking advantage of the rebellion, many Congressmen lectured Jai about a representative government. Although that was far from coming, Jai called for Jamna Lal Bajaj, the president of the Praja Mandal. In April 1939, he relieved Prime Minister Sir Beauchamp of office and appointed Tod. Unfortunately, Tod's tenure lasted only two months. He was the last British prime minister of Jaipur.

Raja Gyan Nath succeeded him, but he proved unfit for the job.

Although, Jai's initial relationship with the Praja Mandal was cordial (primarily owing to Jai's personal equation with Pandit Heera Lal Shastri who was at Mayo when Jai was also there), the relationship soured later. The Public Societies Registration Act was passed which required all societies to be registered. The Praja Mandal refused to get itself registered. It was, therefore, banned, and Jamna Lal Bajaj was prohibited from entering Jaipur. He was intercepted thrice while attempting to come to Jaipur and was sent back. Freddie Young, the irrepressible inspector general of police, wanted him arrested but Jai intervened. Bajaj continued to make efforts to enter Jaipur. Ultimately, he was arrested in February. This led to a flurry of communication, with news flying between the viceroy and the secretary of state. In fact, the viceroy at one time wrote to the secretary of state that he was doubtful whether this young man (Jai) had any interest in the running of the state or its problems. Jai made himself even more vulnerable to such allegations because having melted the Sikar opposition, he went back to England.

On his return, Jai initiated the Jaipur Unlawful Associations Act primarily to repeal the Public Societies Regulation Act and dispense with compulsory registration. This would have legalized the Praja Mandal. R.S. Thomson, the Jaipur resident, was opposed to this idea. He felt Jai was becoming a little too friendly with Bajaj. However, Thomson's opposition could not travel far owing to the change of resident (Conrad Corfield had taken over). Besides, it was around this time that Jai was severely injured in a plane crash at Bombay in 1939. By the time he recovered, the Praja Mandal had become well entrenched.

Jai, not entirely unnecessarily, was credited for the whole affair. The populace was convinced that he had their interest at heart.

---

1   Most kings are addressed by the name of their state. Here, Sikar implies Rao Raja Kalyan Singh of Sikar.

THE THIRD MARRIAGE

Even while the imbroglio in Sikar was creating palpable tensions all over Rajputana, Jai was restless. He was in touch with Gayatri regularly through letters. There was a brief rough patch when the Cooch Behar family realized that the juvenile fascination, which they had thought would disappear, had continued. Jai wrote to her from Bombay on 15 January 1939.

Bombay
15 Jan 1939

Darling Pat

It was a heavenly surprise receiving your letter today… but I don't know if it makes me miserable or happy. I am really at a loss to understand it and all what you mean in it. Before I answer your questions will you be frank and tell me that you really do trust me and believe me to be sincere to you. To know the truth from you would set my mind at ease because when I am with you, you are totally different to when behind my back and away from me. What does really come over you, and I wonder if you really mean what you put in the letter. Really darling, I am feeling too miserable now to write anything but on hearing from you,

I promise I will write and tell you everything, not that I have ever
hidden things from you... I wish to God you were here and I could
talk to you.

Your miserable
Jai

The pressure from the family continued. Although Ma and the
entire family were fond of Jai, they did not relish the idea of
Gayatri being a third wife. However, for Gayatri, being Jai's
wife was all that mattered. Jai's need for Gayatri was clear
from his letters. He wrote to her on 5 March 1939:

5 March 1939

Beloved Pat

The viceroy's visit kept us all very busy so I hope darling, you will
forgive my not writing to you. But what has kept you busy? Are you
up to any good or not darling?! Thank God, the viceroy's visit went
off quite well... I had an awful time on the banquet night having to
make that long speech and I was pissing in my pants till I had a few
drinks before facing the ordeal. Then all went well.
    ...all my love, beautiful and I think of you every second of
my life.

Yours forever
Jai

Ma had rented a house in the Kashmir valley in April 1939. As
soon as the house was done up, Jai arrived in September,
ostensibly to pay a formal visit to the Maharaja of Kashmir.
Once the courtesies were dispensed with, Jai shifted in with
the Cooch Behar household. Shikar trips, bear hunts, picnics

and morning rides filled the days. Gayatri recollects this brief period 'as the last idyll of my girlhood'. Jai had to return to Jaipur since war was imminent. Although India was beyond the periphery, Britain was fully involved and had no larger reservoir of manpower than Hindustan. India had its role to play, even though it was consigned to the background and remained inconspicuous.

Jai's ebullient nature made him vulnerable to accidents. In November 1939, his plane crashed in Bombay, when a vulture flew into its wings and the plane had a free fall for 400 feet. The pilot was killed on the spot, and Jai broke both his ankles. Being the maharaja of an important state of Rajputana, he was well attended to, under the watchful supervision of Sir Roger Lumley, the governor of Bombay. Gayatri was in Srinagar, when the accident took place. The cable said that he was unconscious and dangerously ill. In her words:

> I thought my heart had stopped beating. I had often read in romantic novels how the heroine's heart missed a beat in any highly charged emotional situation, but I never expected to feel this improbable reaction myself. It was then, for the first time, that I fully realized how deeply I loved him. That night I couldn't sleep. Instead, I sat up, miserable, not crying but unable to think of anything but Jai and how much I wanted to be with him. Ma was very sympathetic but made it clear that it was impossible for an unmarried girl to go to Bombay alone. The following day a telegram arrived to say that, although he was seriously ill, he had been pronounced out of immediate danger.

When Jai shifted to Jaipur, Ma went to see him. Gayatri was summoned on a special request from Jai. She spent two days at Jaipur, providing the much needed solace. They parted with promises to write to each other every day. Later, Jai went to Calcutta for the polo season. Before returning, he discussed the marriage with Ma. Gayatri was permitted to be a spectator in the discussion for the first time. Jai used all his charm and persuasion to convince Ma that even though the two years of the cooling-down period, as decided earlier, were not over, the war had accelerated events and, therefore, the marriage schedule also required a change. Seeing his single-minded stubbornness, Ma relented to the marriage within one year. Jai then presented a diamond ring to Gayatri with instructions not to reveal it. They decided she would put it on only at night.

Later, Jai met Ma again at Delhi and persuaded her that the marriage could not wait for even one year. Ma had no choice but to accede again. However, the plan had to be kept a secret till Jai informed his family. Being a maharaja, he had to carry out certain diplomatic manoeuvres to convince the nobility and his relatives of a third marriage. Nonetheless, the date was tentatively fixed for 17 April 1940.

Jai ostensibly gave a party to Second Her Highness to cheer her up when he broke the news that he was going to marry Gayatri. Whether her spirits could have been cheered by this novel method is for the reader to discern.

The apprehensions in Gayatri's family continued. Ila thought that Gayatri, always 'spineless' in Jai's presence, would not be able to deal with his flirtatious nature. Inderjeet teased her saying that Jai, his hero, had got stuck to a 'broomstick'. Ma thought that Gayatri would be 'the latest addition to the Jaipur nursery'. Bhaiya (Gayatri's elder brother) was the only one who had a serious discussion with Gayatri, warning her that Jai was attracted to women and that Gayatri should reconcile herself to his ways without making a scene. The conversation best reveals the situation in Gayatri's own words in *A Princess Remembers*:

He (Bhaiya) tried to make things clear to me, using himself as an example. 'You know I've got a lot of girlfriends—nothing serious—but men often do. And Jai also likes girls. Just because he marries you, you can't expect him to give up all his girls.'

I remember being indignant. 'I certainly will expect it. After all, if he marries me, why does he need all those other girls?'

'Listen,' Bhaiya said patiently, 'the war's on. Jai or I might be sent anywhere. When I go to a new place and meet new girls, I like to go out with them. Jai isn't going to stop liking girls or taking them out just because he's married to you. And really, you mustn't mind.'

'But I will mind.'

'But you mustn't—he isn't trying to hurt you.'

'I can't believe that. If I'm his wife, where's the necessity for outside girlfriends? '

'Do listen, Ayesha. I'm not a bad man, am I? I wouldn't willingly hurt anybody?'

'No, of course not.'

'But do you see that I might continue to have girlfriends even if I were married?'

'You're different,' I said, knowing in a sisterly way that Bhaiya would never change his habits, but refusing to accept that Jai might be the same.

Bhaiya, in exasperation, almost shouted at me. 'But do remember Jai is also a man. He has lots of girlfriends. It doesn't mean anything.'

'Then why shouldn't I be like that, too?' I asked resentfully, knowing that I was so besotted with Jai that I couldn't possibly think of outside flirtations.

'No, no,' Bhaiya seemed almost shocked, 'Girls are different.'

'They certainly are,' I agreed warmly. 'When Jai is away, I'll miss him and probably mope about it.'

'But men don't do that. Please understand. Jai may love you and want to marry you, but that has nothing to do with his being attracted to other girls. Men are like that. It doesn't mean anything.'

I said, 'To me it would mean a lot. I'd hate it.'

Bhaiya sighed deeply and started his lecture all over again. Jai, he explained, was naturally warm-hearted and demonstrative. He couldn't help showing this, and–let's face it–he did like women, and he was attracted to them as they were to him. I continued to insist that none of this would be true after we were married; he loved me and nothing would persuade him to stray, no matter how many women flung themselves at him. Bhaiya said, in a despairing voice, 'Don't say I didn't warn you.'

Even then, behind my protests, somewhere I knew Bhaiya was right and in fact, after we were married, Jai and I used to have flaming rows about his casual habit of saying 'Hello, Beautiful' or 'How's my Wonder Girl?' to women that we knew, and giving them a kiss on the cheek. These quarrels always ended with my saying huffily, 'It's no use, I simply don't understand.'

It may be interesting to note that there were a lot of different reasons for the opposition to Jai's third marriage. The Rajput chieftains objected on the ground of Cooch Behar being inferior in status to Jaipur. In fact, Sir B.J. Glancy (political advisor to Y.S. Roy) held that 'though they (Cooch Behar)[2] described themselves as Kshatriya, they would have great difficulty in establishing their claim to this distinction.' However, on this account, Jai had history with him.

Mirza Raja Man Singh had married Kshama Devi from Cooch Behar more than 400 years ago. The objection, therefore, did not survive. It was also feared that the two senior maharanis would be relegated to the background. Since the Jaipur and Jodhpur households were intimately linked through marriage over a long time, intrusion by an outsider was obviously resented. In fact, they even represented this to Viceroy Lord Linlithgow. The viceroy spoke to Jai. In tune with the times, (King Edward VI) Jai preferred deposition to postponement of his marriage (for the woman he loved). The viceroy was helpless.

While the opposition to the marriage was nearly unanimous, nobody could tell Jai this to his face. There were only two exceptions, Jai's father from Isarda and Amar Singh, and even they did not count for much under the circumstances. Hence, in the end, Jai prevailed. The marriage was on. The subtle art of diplomacy had to be creatively engaged to ensure a respectable congregation for the *barat*. Jai himself went to Udaipur to exert more persuasion on the maharana, since the whole of Rajputana used to look towards him for the lead. Jai later wrote to Udaipur:

> ...The relations existing between our royal houses have always been of the most cordial nature and I am so glad that after this recent visit of mine they have been cemented still further...
>
> I have invariably looked up to Your Highness for advice. The guidance which I received from you and the assurance given by Your Highness have strengthened me considerably. I could not expect a greater practical proof of Your Highness's goodwill towards my person and my house...
>
> With kindest regards,
> Man Singh

The Maharana of Udaipur wrote that he would come for the wedding, if he felt better. The maharana ultimately sent two representatives. In a manner, this put a seal of approval on the marriage. Even while opposition was contained, the British still wanted nothing to do with the marriage and there were instructions in writing, forbidding anyone from attending it. If good wishes had to be conveyed, these had to be prefaced by stating that the wishes were offered in a private capacity. Even Gayatri was aware of the matter. She says in her book:

> I knew that my marriage was not popular with Jai's relatives and the Jaipur nobility. The other two maharanis were related to most of the Rajput princely families, but I was a total outsider.

Notwithstanding the brouhaha, the marriage was on. Despite the war, it was celebrated with customary ostentation. Unfortunately, at this time, Ma's favourite brother, Dhairyashil slipped on the stairs and succumbed to a skull injury in hospital. The Baroda party, already in Cooch Behar, had to return for the funeral. Gayatri had not yet recovered from a recent bout of diphtheria. The wedding, thus, had to be postponed, and 9 May was fixed as the next most auspicious day.

Jai and 40 nobles arrived to a 19-gun salute. Immediately, in Cooch Behar after the arrival of the *barat*, Jai called Ma asking if he could come over for a drink before lunch but permission was refused. No such liberties could be allowed at a wedding attended by a plethora of religious rituals. Welcome arches had been erected along the entire road for the *barat* procession. All the public and private buildings in Cooch Behar were illuminated for the occasion. A hockey match with Jai and Bhaiya captaining opposite sides and special fireworks were also organized.

After the ceremony was over, Jai and Gayatri had to touch everyone's feet including that of Inderjeet, who was younger to Jai. While doing so, Jai muttered *sotto voce*, 'For the first and the last time.' Gayatri received a lot of presents, the most notable being a black Bentley from the Nawab of Bhopal, a two-seated Packard from one of the Jaipur nobles and a house in Mussoorie from Ma's mother.

Although celebrations continued in Cooch Behar for one more week, Jai and Gayatri set off for their honeymoon to Ooty. Ooty was the second choice after Sri Lanka, which had to be overlooked because of the war. Inderjeet came to see them off at Calcutta. This journey was to give Gayatri the first unpleasant taste of purdah. The windows of the entire train were covered with curtains.

At Ooty, Jai and Gayatri stayed in the annexe of Jodhpur House. Gayatri celebrated her 21st birthday while on her honeymoon. This was also the place where she got her first scolding; she had tried to remain in the background and had not escorted her guests to the door. Jai was not one bit reticent about communicating his disapproval. 'What's the matter with you?' he said. 'Your mother has such beautiful manners. Anyone would think you might have picked up some points from her. Who the hell do you think you are to stay behind in the drawing-room and not go to the door to see your guests off?'

Jai soon left for Bangalore for the polo season, leaving Gayatri behind. She later drove down to Bangalore where Second Her Highness was also in town with the children: Bhawani Singh (Bubbles), who was nine years then; Mickey, 11; and Second Her Highness's children, seven-year-old Joey and three-year-old Pat. After the polo tournament, Jai and Gayatri returned to Jaipur by train via Sawai Madhopur. En route, Jai showed Gayatri his native place, Isarda.

Gayatri was fearful while approaching Jaipur, since she was an outsider and fully aware of the suppressed resentment of the nobility, most of whom were related to the first two wives of Jai. She says:

> The nearer we drew to Jaipur, the more terrified and unsure I became. I tried desperately not to show it, but Jai, I think, understood how I felt. As we entered the station, the servants pulled down the blinds around our carriage and very gently Jai told me to cover my face.

Immediately on arrival, Jai's sisters from Isarda, the Maharani of Panna and the wife of Rao Ajit Singh of Jodhpur, accorded a traditional welcome at Viman Bhawan (the railway platform reserved for the arrival of special guests). The newly weds had to first go to the temple of Shila Devi in Amber. In Ram Bagh, Jai had had his own rooms done up for Gayatri and shifted himself to a nearby suite. Jai's first wife, who largely led a non-obtrusive existence, had begun living at Jodhpur and used to stay in City Palace whenever she was in Jaipur. Second Her Highness stayed in Ram Bagh Palace most of the time. Gayatri, although allotted her own space in the zenana in City Palace, preferred to stay in Ram Bagh.

An unending string of soirées commenced and continued, which required Gayatri to change frequently. Removing ivory bangles everyday became an ordeal and in Gayatri's words, 'Jai who was far gentler than any of my maids, would do it for me.' Jai took Gayatri on a conducted tour of City Palace from where he showed her the temple of Govind Dev in whose name the Kings of Jaipur ruled their state. The zenana quarters at that time had 400 ladies, including widows, relatives, servants, attendants, ladies in waiting, maids, and cooks. One of Madho Singh's widows, Ma Sahiba Tanwar, was still alive. When she arrived in Jaipur, Gayatri could speak only Bengali and English. Wisely, Jai did not encourage her to learn the dialect. Thus, Gayatri was kept aloof and *ipso facto* insulated from intrigues and vulnerability to rumours.

Whenever Jai was out of Jaipur, his elder brother Bahadur Singh was deputed to accompany Gayatri for the morning rides. Second Her Highness was only 24 when Gayatri got married. Besides an age difference of only three years, she was also the only person with whom Gayatri could converse. Being the niece of the famous cricketer Ranjit Singh of Jamnagar (after whom the Ranji Trophy is named), Second Her Highness was also more exposed to life than the Rajput ladies of the time. Yet, the seclusion from men was so complete that even a doctor had to get information on the ailment through a messenger. The thermometer used to be sent to the doctor through a maid. This method was gainfully employed by sending a thermometer dipped in hot water to the doctor to avoid boring official engagements.

Gayatri was taken on a tour of the surrounding forts, too. She mentions visiting one fort,[3] which they reached after a long and tortuous climb, where the fabulous Jaipur treasure was supposed to be housed. Only Jai was allowed inside, and Gayatri had to wait outside. Jai never told Gayatri anything regarding the treasure.

Motidoongari, another small fort near Ram Bagh, was later renovated when Gayatri took a fancy to it. It became the favoured haunt for both of them for quiet lunches and dinners with intimate friends.

Gayatri gradually got used to the pace of Jai's life which, in addition to regal duties, was primarily dictated by the polo seasons and summer jaunts to London.

---

1   Some people jokingly referred to it as Jai's eight-year itch. His first marriage was in 1924, the second in 1932, and the third in 1940. However, by 1948, the scenario had changed dramatically.

2   Cooch Behar and Bhutan were earlier part of the kingdom of Kamrup, which subsequently fragmented. The Bhutanese king captured the Maharaja of Cooch Behar. An appeal was made to East India Company (Warren Hastings) in 1773. The intervention of even the Dalai Lama of Tibet was sought, and the king was finally released. A British resident was placed here in 1788.

3   It was the Nahargarh Fort which was customarily guarded bu the Meenas. In 1942, there was a mishap. A seal of one part of the treasury was found broken. All the Meena guards were arrested. The episode was kept a secret but, thereafter, the public and private treasure was reorganized. The public treasure was moved from Nahargarh to Jaigarh. Jai's personal treasure was shifted to the Kapad Dwara in City Palace. Half of it was sent to Bombay to be sold under the care of Raja Atal, the finance minister. Shares were purchased from the accruals. In 1947, the remainder of Jai's personal treasure was moved from Kapad Dwara to Motidoongari.

WARTIME

The commencement of the Second World War changed the complexion of life in Jaipur. When the war was declared, Jai sent a letter to the viceroy to seek the king's permission to join the Life Guards. When the viceroy himself interdicted, Jai approached Buckingham Palace directly, placing his personal services at the disposal of 'My Beloved Sovereign'. The sovereign also refused. Even that did not prevent Jai from continuing his efforts to somehow or the other join the war.

Before the war, Jai had reorganized the Jaipur State Forces. The Kachhwaha Horse, raised in 1922, was reorganized in 1939. It was used for quelling the 'HUR' disturbance in 1942–1944. The Sawai Man Guard was initially raised as the body of guards for Raja Man Singh, the Commander-in-Chief of Akbar. It was called Khasa Risala. The name changed to Khasa-Chowki-Sardar, then to Bada Risala, and again to Risala Kalan. In 1932, Sawai Man Singh trained it on the lines of the Brigade of Guards and gave it the present name, the Sawai Man Guards. It was renamed 17 Rajputana Rifles after 1947. The 1st Jaipur infantry was raised in 1923 by reorganizing the old Tilangan Jaipur, which had fought the battles of Kabul and Kandhar. These outfits were ready for battle. First, the Jaipur infantry was sent to the Middle East and then the Sawai Man Guards to the north-west frontier on the border of Afghanistan.

The Rajput Sabha had pleaded with Jai to keep himself away from war or at the very least accompany the Jaipur troops if joining was unavoidable. But Jai was not moved. Quentin Crewe writes that all along, Jai never made any effort to join the unit that he had raised. That can probably be understood better if we peep into the psyche of the rulers. Britain was the governing nation with the king at the helm. Ordinary Britishers who moved in the social circle of the maharajas, were considered superior to the local nobles. The maharajas, therefore, had a close and intimate association with the Britishers. The local people, including the nobility were considered inferior, although there was no conspicuous manifestation of such an attitude. While there was still a concern for and attachment with the local troops, that was all, and no more. It is something like the relationship between the officer and jawan in the army. The officer is supposed to look after the welfare of a jawan. However, the jawan provides no companionship to the officer. Jai, therefore, did not desire to go into the theatre of war on the lofty throne of a king.

Jai's assiduous efforts to join the war were rewarded, when in September 1940, Jai was attached to 13 Lancers at Risalpur. Gayatri accompanied him for a few months and they lived the life of a young army couple for some time. Jai was a captain. However, the Maharaja Captain had a retinue of six servants in addition to *sayeeses* for Jai's ponies. There was riding, squash and entertainment at the club. Jai would come home in the evening and recount the day's events to Gayatri.

She, in turn, would give him the radio news, recorded in short hand, putting to use her secretarial training in college. The bliss, however, was short-lived and ended when the regiment had to move to the border. The wives were asked to stay behind. On Jai's insistence, Gayatri had to return to Jaipur to a lonely Christmas.

Jai was granted an emergency commission in the Household Cavalry, in April 1941, the first Indian to be so honoured. He thanked King George VI profusely, and returned for celebrations in Jaipur. Later, he set sail from Bombay for the Middle East on 9 May to join the Household Cavalry. May 9 was also his first wedding anniversary. Gayatri saw him off to the warfront, within one year of the marriage. She was the only one who did not oppose his endeavour to join the war effort. As Jai said, 'A wonderful girl and the best companion one could ever seek.'

The best laid plans of mice and men and maharajas can go awry. When Jai arrived in the Middle East, his regiment had already left. He was, therefore, attached to the Royal Scots Greys at Gaza. Shortly, thereafter he came to Cairo as a liaison officer with the Indian State Forces. Within the Indian Army, he was a major general. Simultaneously, he carried the rank of temporary captain of the Life Guards. This created a piquant situation. Whenever Jai wore the Life Guards uniform, he had to salute majors and superior ranks. But while on duty with the Indian Army as a major general, he was saluted by the same persons whom he had saluted the previous day.

The war also saw Gayatri working in a different role. She and Second Her Highness organized parties for knitting and stitching socks and sweaters. They organized plays and fêtes to raise money for the troops at the front. The English comptroller of Ram Bagh had just left, so Gayatri took over this job, which resulted in massive savings. The comptroller's task was to order the stores, maintain store rooms, draw menus and look after everyday needs, including the kitchen staff, uniforms, the household linen, etc. In addition, the royal household had a military secretary, in charge of the buildings, grounds, gardens, cars, and catering to the needs of the guests. An entirely separate set of people was earmarked to organize shikar. General Bhairon Singh used to look after the tents, camp furniture, and outdoor equipment. Col. Keshari Singh was in charge of guns and other shooting equipment. Interestingly, both were at loggerheads. Gayatri intervened to resolve their differences, but her efforts proved futile. In addition, Gayatri utilized wartime to try and draw the Rajputana ladies out of the purdah system. However, results were not commensurate with the efforts she put in.

Meanwhile, the series of polo accidents and air mishaps Jai had suffered showed their effect. Jai was pronounced medically unfit in August. A reluctant Jai had to head home within four months of his going to the front.

A Village Panchayat Act and a Municipal Act were promulgated around this time to give fulfilment to the aspirations of the people. Jai's deep desire to get to the front again was punctuated now with a desire to do well for his people. The Panchayat Act gave administrative functions to local bodies, thus, ensuring protection for the poor. The Municipal Act gave scope for half the seats to be filled through the elections.

As a king, Jai was now getting into the fast-forward mode. He wrote:

I would add that while I have the keenest personal desire to get to the front again, and play a more active part than is possible here, I well realize how important is the effort towards victory that can be made at home. Neither in men nor in any sort of contribution shall we be found to fall short. No state understands better than Jaipur that the single duty of working, in all ways, for speedy victory requires all our energies and resources. While, like the Government of India and the Army itself, we have also been looking beyond victory and endeavouring to prepare for the future, we well know that the immediate demands of war are paramount and shall allow no others to compete with them. Nor is this a mere matter of duty to us.

It was at this time that Gayatri got the idea of starting a school for girls. While girls from middle-class families were taking to education, the daughters of the nobles were still observing purdah. She, therefore, started the Maharani Gayatri Devi School, appointing Miss Lilian Donnithorne Lutter as the first principal. Miss Lutter was from Edinburgh and had taught in Burma for a few years before the war. The school began in 1943 with 40 students. Its reputation has, over the years, travelled across the globe.

Jai had appointed Mirza Ismail[1] as his prime minister in June 1941. Mirza Ismail actively pursued sweeping reforms in every aspect of Jaipur life. Jaipur was getting overcrowded and dirty. Mirza Ismail removed all encroachments, restored constructions to the lines drawn by Sawai Jai Singh, and repainted the houses in pink as was done in the time of Ram Singh II. Temples located in the middle of the road were removed, diplomatically, by moving them to more suitable locations. Cecil Beaton, a friend of Jai, visited Jaipur around this time and wrote in *Vogue*:

> Sir Mirza is the arch enemy of corrugated iron sheets, brass hands and of almost everything else that is crude and vulgar...Already the metamorphosis he has achieved in such a short time is incredible, but his plans are as countless as his aspirations. The legacy of this

wonderful city has fallen into safe hands. The Maharaja of Jaipur is
a young man with a proud appreciation of the beauties of his State
and a keen interest in building anew.

Jai had made a perfect choice. Mirza Ismail had a passion for
progress. While addressing the *nazirs* and *tehsildars* of Jaipur
State on 21 November 1942, Mirza said:

> It should be our constant aim and earnest endeavour to promote the
> happiness and prosperity of the people of the State in every way
> open to us and to attain for the administration a high place among
> the administrations in India. This is His Highness's ambition and it
> is up to us to enable him to realize it. His Highness is above all most
> anxious to improve the economic condition of his people, the
> standard of living...

Mirza Ismail had come from Mysore and had worked under
an enterprising maharaja. He put all his experience and
learning to good use in Jaipur. Construction activities,
renovation, removal of encroachments, and various
progressive activities were begun. Jai would regularly go
around checking on the progress. He used to fly around the
city in his Gipsy Moth. One day, one of the propellers fell off,
but he was unhurt. Jai had a boyhood enthusiasm for visiting
places of development, like a man possessed, at any odd hour.
The places, which were as sacrosanct as royal shoots, were
sold at 25 paise per square yard to the public. Jai took a
special delight in laying foundation stones, cutting ribbons,
and declaring public places open. The idea of building a Man
Palace to rival the Ummaid Bhawan Palace (built by the
Maharaja of Jodhpur) fleetingly crossed his mind but was
never put into action. Blomfield, who had earlier constructed
the shooting lodges at Ramgarh and Sawai Madhopur, built
the Jaipur House in Delhi at this time. Jai used to attend all
the meetings of the council of ministers but on Sir Mirza's

suggestion, he stopped doing so to keep himself above any controversy.

The council was gradually broadened and common people were included. The first move towards democratization commenced with a proclamation on 1 January 1944 for the establishment of two representative bodies, a Legislative Council and a Representative Assembly. In fact, Sir Mirza was tolerant of the Praja Mandal activities also. He would tell them: 'Go ahead and demonstrate, strike and parade to your heart's content. I shall not stop you as long as you really remain non-violent according to the Congress programme. There will be no repression and no terrorism in Jaipur.'

When Pandit Heera Lal Shastri wrote to Sir Mirza Ismail on 16 September 1942 regarding the Praja Mandal's plan to hold an agitation in Jaipur, Sir Mirza replied promptly a day later:

> Your letters gave me a rude shock. They distressed me. I fear pardon my saying so, you have not acted with sufficient foresight or in the best interest of the state and the country in general. I may be wrong, of course, but that is my conviction. My conscience is perfectly clear; and so is my duty. But I wish such a situation had not arisen at all. It will only hamper me in my work for the betterment of the people of Jaipur and interfere with the realization of a dream I have been dreaming for them! Let me appeal to you and your party even at this late hour to think and think again before taking the plunge. I wish most fervently that you could even now be persuaded to abandon the idea of starting an agitation in this state, especially when things are quieting down in other states and even in British India. Let us be realistic. A vast gulf divides realities from mere emotionalism.
>
> **P.S.:** I should like to see you and any of your friends that you might like to bring along and have a heart-to-heart talk with you. Believe me I am as ardent a nationalist as any of you.[2]

With this kind of dispensation, there were hardly any lathi charges or firing and obviously there was no rancour among the people for the authorities or the royalty.

All the progress that was taking place was not to the liking of the British, since they felt that the money spent on these projects should be devoted to the war effort. Advice by the political department to postpone expenditure on public work was cheekily ignored. Jai wrote back saying that he would undertake no new work that was not vital. This insouciance was not appreciated, leading to repercussions which were petty. Effort was made to discredit Sir Mirza. An issue was made out of the word 'royal salute' used in the ceremonials at Jaipur.

Nevertheless, Jai and Sir Mirza's efforts did not waver. The good work of Sir Mirza Ismail stood the test of time. The main road of Jaipur was named after him and is popularly known today as MI Road. A distinguished American editor had come to Jaipur in the early forties, when Jai and Sir Mirza Ismail were carrying out sweeping reforms in Jaipur. He remarked: 'For those who are inclined to wonder whether India has the capacity to govern and develop herself, here is a blunt answer.'

In 1943, Udaipur invited Jodhpur and Jaipur for a visit. Customarily, the Maharana of Udaipur took precedence over the Maharajas of Jodhpur and Jaipur. Udaipur's purdah system was not only intact, but more crushingly so. Ladies led a separate existence and would not join the men for any function whatsoever. This was Gayatri's first visit to Udaipur, and she had carried a camera with her. It turned out to be unnecessary baggage since the ladies travelled in heavily cloistered purdahs. The formalities in the men's section were as extreme. Whilst taking drinks, everyone was supposed to follow the maharana, sip by sip. Jai was unaware of this and

would have been embarrassed had the Maharaja of Jodhpur
not brought it to his notice.

Jai's first wife died on 25 December 1944. She was only
45. Bubbles (who was 13 years old), Mickey, Joey and Pat
were at a shooting camp. Jai's first wife had been a loner
from the beginning and her death did not change the pace of
events in any manner. The funeral was organized the next day
while the development of Jaipur continued apace and
uninterrupted.

Sir Mirza Ismail noted in his autobiography, *My Public
Life,* 'In these times had it not been for the strong support of
the maharaja, I should have left Jaipur.' He called Jai 'an
enlightened ruler who true to his promise gave him full
support.' Sir Mirza said, 'What I liked most in Jaipur was
freedom from intrigue. His Highness would not allow any
intrigue of any kind to raise its ugly head where he was
concerned. He formed his own judgment, uninfluenced by
busybodies and acted upon it.'

Jai was finally pronounced fit for army service again in
August 1942. He was asked to join the Staff College at
Quetta. He made another request for a posting to the front,
but was politely ignored.

Despite a progressive ruler and a flourishing state, it
may come as a bit of a surprise that Jaipur had practically
no factories in 1940. And this, in the face of the fact that
the Shekhawati region, which was under Jaipur, was the
birthplace of the Marwaris, the richest businessmen in
Calcutta and Bombay—the Birlas, Bajajs, Piramals, the
Goenkas, the Poddars, *et al.* In fact, the Birlas had established
an Intermediate College at Pilani, which was inaugurated
by Jai. Subsequently, this college was given a degree status
and it became the Birla Institute of Technology & Science

(BITS). Many leading lights of Silicon Valley in the US are from this institution. The Rolling and Spinning Mills and the Metal and Electrical Works factory were established in Jaipur.

Jai was dividing his time between army and state duties. Till 1943, he continued at the Staff College. However, he did not enjoy his work much, which is clear from a letter to Gayatri:

> After two days of bloody hard work and walking about on these beastly hills, my legs have given way... the food is bloody but the bar is a good saving grace... It's been raining here since we arrived and bloody cold. I wish you were here darling to warm me up. No rugs can keep the cold out but your arms.

In 1944, Jai was allowed to go abroad for liaison work with the Indian State Forces. His visit to encourage the Indian troops and sort out the difficulties along with the British Commanders proved embarrassing because the Indian troops would give him an enthusiastic welcome and ignore the senior general. Jai also renewed his contacts with old friends, like Lord Roderick Pratt and the Duke of Wellington.

Jai's mother from Isarda died in 1945. It was a shattering blow for Jai. A truncated childhood, happy if incomplete memories, and the nostalgia of his young days were to stay with Jai for all time to come. He used to write sentimental letters to his mother about keeping *puri* and pickles when he returned from Woolwich. He would go to his birthplace to bathe in the River Banas to get the feel of his boyhood days. Much had happened since Jai was adopted but childhood memories endured these kaleidoscopic changes. Chand recollects that Jai used to regularly visit Isarda during the annual shikar camps at Sawai Madhopur. His mother's death left a vacuum in Jai's life.

Meanwhile, the progressive reforms taking place in Jaipur were for all to see. As Sir Mirza Ismail observed while addressing the assembly:

> The new reforms have brought Jaipur State in line with the most advanced Indian States. The proceedings of the last four days have convinced me that the high laurels that the subjects of His Highness the Maharaja have won in outer fields—in the field of commerce and industry, on the field of battle—will also be won by you in the quieter field of the administration of the state.

Even the ladies actively participated in the Representative Assembly. The prime minister, during his address at the closing of the first assembly session, observed:

> I should thank the lady members for the intelligent and helpful part they have taken in the proceedings, especially, as is natural, in matters concerning the fair sex. A community whose women are wide awake need not despair of progress. Though this was the first session of the Assembly, I would like to think that it has sufficiently demonstrated to you the practical value of this body and its potentialities for the future. The Assembly is, indeed, a unique institution, based as it is upon the oriental conception of democracy and designed to give an impetus to the growing political consciousness of the people, such as the more formal councils cannot give by providing a forum for the free exchange of views between the government and the representatives of the people on matters essential to the life of the community.

While addressing the joint session of the Representative Assembly and Legislative Council on 17 September 1945, Sir Mirza Ismail said:

> In sanctioning these far-reaching constitutional changes (for far-reaching they are, whatever some critics may say) His Highness the Maharaja has granted to his people a measure of political reforms whose value will become more and more manifest with the passage

of time. These changes, I may remind you, have brought the State of Jaipur, so far as constitutional government is concerned, in line with the most advanced states in India. It required courage and imagination on the part of His Highness to take so great a step forward in a State where representative institutions have been non-existent for all practical purposes. I have no doubt that His Highness's wisdom will be fully justified and that his generosity will be amply rewarded in the gratitude and love of his people. The machinery that has been set in motion does not by any means represent the consummation of democracy. It represents, however, a bold advance on the road which leads to the goal of popular government.

Crewe says:

As a person, the Maharaja of Jaipur was charming, handsome and wholly lacking in any of the disagreeable characteristics that have been attributed to the princes of India. He was not an intellectual, nor a great political reformer by inclination; he was primarily a sportsman and a soldier. The circumstances of his reign, however, brought out in him unexpected qualities and it intrigued me to trace the development of a rather innocent and simple character into a man of wisdom and stature.

By the time Sir Mirza completed his four years in office, the University of Rajputana had been established in Jaipur. Jai had gradually metamorphosed from being an English maharaja to a devoted king.

---

1   Amin-ul-Mulk, Sir Mirza M. Ismail, K.C.I.E, O.B.E., had been administrator with the Maharaja of Mysore for 33 years, the last 15 of which were as Dewan. He attended all three round table conferences, first as representative of the southern States (Mysore, Travancore, Cochin, and Pudukotta), the second on behalf of Mysore, Jaipur and Jodhpur, and third, the sittings of the Joint Parliamentary Committee on behalf of Mysore.

2   There was a Gentlemen's Agreement between the Praja Mandal and the Jaipur Government. According to Pandit Heera Lal Shastri, the principal terms of the agreement were:

(i) That the people of Jaipur would be free to agitate within the state against British Imperialism and even against the war effort.

(ii) That the Jaipur authorities would not arrest any person (whether he was a resident of Jaipur or even an outsider) taking part in the struggle in British India if he or she came to Jaipur, and that the Government of Jaipur would take immediate steps to establish responsible government in the state. For the Praja Mandal's part, it was agreed that there would be no agitation against the Maharaja of Jaipur, who had agreed to come halfway to meet the wishes of the people of the State.

INDEPENDENCE AND THE AFTERMATH

The end of the war was greeted with jubilation the world over. Jai donated 200 pounds for the restoration of the Guard's Chapel and a 1000 pounds to the Life Guards. He eagerly claimed the ribbons and medals of every theatre of war that he had visited.

Life at Jaipur returned to full princely glory. Jai was now 35 and had already been on the throne for 24 years. He put the lessons of war to good use. Jai had raised an army unit in 1942 in imitation of the Life Guards and named it the Rajendra Hajari Guards. Regular parades were now held. Gayatri's efforts to draw the women out of purdah were at their aggressive best. A ladies club on the outskirts of Ramniwas Bagh was made functional. Sneh Govind Singh[1] recollects that Gayatri was gradually becoming an icon. All the ladies used to try to copy her style in every possible way. Earlier, the gatherings in the evenings used to be exclusively a male affair. Gayatri changed all that. The Rajput ladies were very much part of the social evenings held in private homes. Ashok Club, the hub of all social activities and the ideal place to gather for the latest news and gossip, was, however, still a male preserve.

Lord Wavell visited Jaipur in 1946. He passed through the heart of the city, interrupted only by the showering of flowers on his car. Yet Wavell's report to King George VI was not complimentary. Wavell claimed that '...(Jai) takes very little interest in the affairs of the state. On all state matters, he referred me to his Prime Minister Sir Mirza Ismail...' He had some uncomplimentary things to say about Jai even to the political advisor. Even earlier, commenting on Jai's participation in North Africa consequent to his commissioning, Wavell had said: 'He came to Cairo early in the war to join the Life Guards, who were then in the Iraq desert, and preferred to remain in Cairo, nominally attached to the Scots Greys but really doing little.' Wavell, being a puritan, had a narrow view of the world. He was unaware of the progress taking place in Jaipur. He also omitted to note that there was no compulsion for Jai to go to the front and that Jai had gone against all advice and persuasion. He, in fact, fought hard to be permitted to join the war effort and that too, within one year of his marriage to Gayatri. But Wavell's string of failures in North Africa, while trying to grapple with Rommel and the bitter experiences of those days, punctuated his psyche and his perceptions. For this reason, his views on the various personalities of the time cannot be given much credence but need to be recorded for posterity, considering that he was a viceroy in India at a time of great change.

Meanwhile, the efforts of the Indian National Congress were bearing fruit and it had become clear to princes all over India (or at least to those who could see) that the days of the Britishers were numbered. The arrival of the Britishers in the early 19th century had sedated the princes at the cost of real power, with their security assured and the future insured. Now however, the security blanket was getting thinner. The voices of the people and their aspirations were becoming shriller, and the necessity to adjust to the new reality was never more dire or urgent. Fortunately, for Jai, the Sikar revolt had jolted him out of his slumber. He had a cordial relationship with the Praja Mandal, which was a pale shadow of the Indian National Congress, in Rajputana. The Praja Mandal thus received a positive response from the administration. The post-war period saw the taming of Churchill. The Labour Government came to power in 1946 and the desperate desire for independence was spurred.

A Constitutional Reforms Committee was set up. The formation of a Legislative Council and Representative Committee earlier were a response to these changed times.

Jai and other princes had already been part of the process, as it evolved in the round table conferences, in the early thirties. In fact, Jaipur, Jodhpur, and Udaipur had sent a joint delegate for the conference. At that point of time, Jai 'considered it essential that the relationship between the Crown of England and his State would remain unaltered and would definitely be provided for in the Constitution'. However, 15 years since the round table conference is a long period in such turbulent and momentous times.

The Chamber of Princes[2] set up a States Negotiation Committee to identify the princes' role in the interim government (the Constituent Assembly). As expected, the princes, lacking exposure to facts as well as realpolitik under the tutelage of the British, were unequal to the task awaiting them. Disagreements and discord were rife. Consequently, the negotiators quite comfortably outfoxed the princes, despite the wherewithal and the strong bonds the princes had with their subjects.

The nawab of Bhopal was the chancellor of the Chamber of Princes. He wanted the princes to wait until the framework of the Constitution was over before joining the proceedings of the Constituent Assembly. On the other hand, Jaipur, Jodhpur, Bikaner, Patiala, and Gwalior were more than anxious to join the deliberations at the earliest opportunity, to be able to partake of power in the new framework. Even historically, Jaipur had always backed Delhi, and they were always on cordial terms. By now, it was clear that the romance with the British Crown was coming to an end, and if loyalties were to be promised, it was to the new dispensation in India and not to the nominal British Head.

The theoretical choice before the princely states was to join either India or Pakistan, or claim independence. However, the geographical location was to dictate the choice almost entirely. Jai himself had never considered the third option. Whether it was an atavistic attachment to Delhi or an eagle eye on the events—perspicacious, discerning and anticipating the future—is difficult to say. Mountbatten recollected later, that even if all the princes had got together and combined their armies, they might have had a chance, but they never worked together. Unity among the princes was the desideratum. And even then, it was a slim possibility.

Viceroy Wavell was equally inadequate to the task at hand. He planned to divide India into various fragments. When Clement Attlee, the prime minister of Britain, announced in February 1947 that India would be given independence in June 1948, Wavell resigned.

Lord Francis Albert Victor Nicholas Mountbatten, Viscount Mountbatten of Burma K.G., P.C., G.M.S.I.,

G.M.I.E., G.C.V.O., K.C.B., (Dicky), then aged 46, took over. The pace of negotiations with the princes gathered momentum with Mountbatten's arrival. Dicky was blue-blooded besides other things, therefore his presence was expected to give a smooth edge to parleys with princes.

However, a walkout by Bikaner from the States Negotiation Committee, had already delivered a body blow to the dream of a separate princely India. Jai, being close to Dicky, was largely nonchalant. His attitude could well have been owing to the realization that independence was ruled out. In a speech delivered at a state banquet, on 13 December 1931, Jai had said:

> I should like to take this opportunity to reaffirm my strong conviction that in a Federation of Provinces and States, the solution of the problem of India's constitutional future is to be found. The picture is not yet complete, but I hope when the details are filled in, it will be such as will be acceptable to all the States and British India.

The attitude of the princes themselves ruled out independence. However, the smaller states were still extremely apprehensive. Jaipur was one of the 18 viable princely states, and Jai had a towering stature. On the other hand, the sense of insecurity and helplessness being faced by the smaller units was almost frightening. A letter written by his brother-in-law, Yadvendra Singh, the Maharaja of Panna, a small state, beseeching him for indulgence, indicates their insecurity:

> My dear Jai,
>
> ...I hope you are not unmindful of the talk we had here about the utter need for some sort of cohesion and unity in Rajputana and the

neighbouring region. The political situation is nearing its climax and the next few months will witness hectic developments...We may find we are faced with a formula not to our liking... At that stage, it may be truly difficult—well nigh impossible to upset the apple cart...

As I said then, I repeat again that you are in that enviable position to give an inspiring lead in regenerating that constructive spirit of mutual understanding and cohesion which would bring about the desired solidarity of Rajputana and its neighbours...

Since Dicky, an upright man, was at the helm, Jai felt safe. Besides, Jai had a good deal in common with Dicky. Polo was one of them. They were both dedicated to the British royal family. Jai and Mountbatten were both keen soldiers and loved the extravaganza of uniform. Both had incisive minds and both loved socializing. The main difference between the two was that Jai was unassuming and a little laid back, while Dicky was aggressive and focused. He did not let the trust placed by the princes on him interfere with the direction of his purpose.

A States Department under Sardar Vallabhbhai Patel was already negotiating with the princely states when Jai returned from London in July 1947. The negotiations with these states acquired importance because even though the combined might of all the armies of the princely states had only an outside chance of putting up any resistance, yet their non-cooperation could be a nightmare. The communication network of the entire country ran through one or the other princely state. If the princes united, the post and telegraph, airways, railways and such essential services could be brought to a standstill. The implications of such a situation materializing were mind-boggling. However, the truculent princes were playing truant for various reasons. V.P. Menon, the secretary to Patel, suggested that the princely states be asked to accede only three aspects, i.e., communications, defence and foreign affairs.[3] At this point of time, accepting the suggestion, Patel assured the princes that their autonomy would be scrupulously respected. As we shall see later, this was one of the many promises that were broken by the new dispensation in the name of democracy and progress. The helpless princes were being led up the garden path. The scythe had moved into action.

Sir Conrad Corfield, earlier a resident at Jaipur, was now on Mountbatten's staff. He was suspected of being sympathetic to the princes and was summarily sacked. Initially, Mountbatten parleyed with the princes individually. He then proposed to Patel that if the new dispensation permitted the princes to retain their titles, privy purses, immunity from arrest, palaces and quasi-diplomatic status, he would try and persuade them to sign the Act of Accession. There were over 550 princes in India. Towards this end, he called a meeting of the chamber of princes on 25 July 1947.

In *Freedom at Midnight,* Larry Collins and Dominique Lapierre have recorded this event:

> It was the last assembly of the world's most exclusive fraternity. Sweating profusely under their brocaded tunics, their decoration covered uniforms, their bejewelled turbans, 75 of the most important maharajas and nawabs of India and dewans representing 74 others, waited in the drenching humidity of a New Delhi summer day to learn from the mouth of the viceroy the fate History held in store for them.

Mountbatten begged them to, 'Look forward ten years and consider what the situation in India and the world will be then, and have the foresight to act accordingly.' 'You are about to face a revolution,' he told them. 'In a very brief moment you will lose forever your sovereignty. It is inevitable. Do not,' he pleaded, 'turn your backs on the India emerging on 15th August. That India will not have enough capable men to represent her overseas.' She was going to need doctors, lawyers, able administrators, and trained officers to replace the British in her army. Many of those princes educated abroad, and experienced in handling the affairs of their states, had skills India would need. They could become playboys on the beaches of the Riviera, or-they could offer their services to the nation and find a new role for themselves and their class in Indian society. He had no doubt which course they should follow. 'Marry the new India,' he begged them.

Jai realized that he had never controlled defence and foreign affairs. There was, therefore, no net loss of control. The new prospect was more tempting in the sense that there was to be a freedom that would be more real. There would be no resident looking over the shoulder, and no viceroy sitting at Delhi, ready to jump at every opportunity to tick the princes off. Even despite the ratiocination, Mountbatten's presence was so reassuring to Jai that even before Independence, he left for England with his sons, Bubbles and Joey. As it turned out, Mountbatten belied the faith placed in him by the princes. However, this important aspect of Dicky's role has never come under scrutiny.

Jai signed the Instrument of Accession on 12 August 1947, whereby Jaipur state acceded to the Dominion of India in respect of external affairs, defence, and communications. Simultaneously, the Jaipur government signed a Standstill Agreement in respect of matters of common concern to the Dominion of India and the State of Jaipur. This was also signed on 12 August 1947.

Sir V.T. Krishnamachari[4] had taken over as prime minister

from Sir Mirza Ismail. An impressive ceremony was held at Ramniwas Garden, where Jai's message to his people was conveyed through Prime Minister V.T. Krishnamachari:

> An Independent India will be called upon to shoulder great responsibilities; and I have every confidence that we in Jaipur will cheerfully assume our share of those responsibilities and assist, with the best that is in us, in the creation of an India which will take its rightful place among the free nations of the world.

Independence on 15 August 1947 was accompanied by a communal conflagration all over India. Fearing that the violence would spread to Jaipur, Jai returned from England immediately. At that time the population of Jaipur was about 2 million, one-tenth of it being Muslim. In those turbulent times, Jai, accompanied by a Muslim colonel, used to tour the city in an open jeep, assuring everyone that they were all his subjects, irrespective of their religion. He warned the Hindus of grave consequences should any Muslim be hurt. It is of some credit to Jai (as also to other Rajputana states) that the madness that engulfed the entire nation, the horror of which continues to benumb even the new generation, was never allowed to touch Jaipur. It was also a fitting reply to the British accusation that Jai was anti-Mohammedan.

Jai learnt through his intelligence agencies that the Pakistani Army was making desperate efforts to seduce the Muslims to cross over to Pakistan and was even trying to wean them away from military service in Jaipur. He wrote a letter to the secretary of the Defence Department, Colonel Mirza:

> I wish to take this opportunity of addressing you in connection with our *Qaimkhanis*.[5] I have been informed very reliably that a Mohammedan Army Officer, formerly of the 18th Cavalry and now reported to be a member of the Pakistan Army, has been actively trying to induce our *Qaimkhanis*, who have lived peacefully for

hundreds of years in this State, to migrate to Pakistan and is dissuading them from joining or supporting the Jaipur State Forces. Knowing you as well as I do, I request you, as a friend to see that such action is definitely discouraged. Should our *Qaimkhanis* have any cause to feel dissatisfied, I would be very glad indeed to look into and redress their complaints, but it pains me considerably to learn that a section of my subjects—who have a record of loyalty second to none and for whom I have the greatest esteem—are being misled and induced to act in a manner prejudicial to the State. I would appreciate it very much if you could very kindly make necessary enquiries and drop me a line to put my mind at rest on this score.

No Muslim left Jaipur. In fact, many Hindus poured into Jaipur from Pakistan, more particularly from Sindh.

December saw the first major celebration in Jaipur after Independence, on the occasion of the Silver Jubilee of Jai's accession to the throne in 1922 (Gayatri's brother Bhaiya had also become a king around the same time and their silver jubilees were celebrated almost within a month of each other). The celebrations were held on a grand scale and continued for weeks together. Fourteen ruling princes visited Jaipur. Jai, Gayatri and Mickey (Jai's eldest daughter) shifted to Motidoongari. Second Her Highness and other ladies shifted to City Palace, leaving Ram Bagh free for the guests. Among the invitees were Lord and Lady Mountbatten, who attended the special durbar in Dewan-i-Am on 14 December 1947. There was a formal banquet where Jai was invested with title of 'Knight Grand Commander of the Most Exalted Order of Star of India (G.C.S.I.)'. Although all the other orders of the Indian Empire had been suspended with Independence, somehow the Star had strangely not been suspended. Mountbatten asked for special permission from the king to invest two maharajas with this honour (the other one was the Maharaja of Bikaner). Bikaner and Jaipur were the only maharajas to call Mountbatten by his Christian name, Dicky. On this memorable occasion, Jai presented a jade-handle dagger to Mountbatten, that had been captured by Raja Man Singh from Afghanistan in 1585. Speaking at the state banquet at Ram Bagh Palace, Governor General Mountbatten said:

As was only to be expected, His Highness the Maharaja of Jaipur, whose state in recent years has been well to the fore in all constitutional and administrative progress, was one of those rulers who took a leading part in bringing about accession.

If I may speak for a moment on Jaipur State itself, I should like to say how much I, personally, and my government appreciate the constitutional and administrative advances which have been made in recent years, and which I feel sure will continue. I think the best evidence of the good political atmosphere in the state is shown by the happy relations that exist everywhere between all sections of His Highness' subjects; the absence of disorders in the state during recent months is a striking tribute to the policy which His Highness' Government has pursued, and I have been particularly interested to see in the streets of Jaipur City, the friendly intermingling of Hindus and Muslims.

On the administrative side, Jaipur has been a leading state for many years, and the fine new buildings which can be seen everywhere, the new university, the magnificent hospital, and the schools, reflect the greatest credit on His Highness, and the policy he and his government have followed.

I have known His Highness intimately for many years, and as he has reminded you earlier, we often met on the polo field, but His Highness's activities have not been confined to the field of sport. He holds the unique privilege of having served as an officer in His Majesty's Household Cavalry, and seen war service with the Life Guards. In addition, the Jaipur Guard's war service in Italy is well known to all of you here, and I shall never forget the privilege and pleasure I had of meeting this fine unit during my visit to Hong Kong in 1945.

Those of us who had the privilege of seeing the Jaipur Guards trooping the Colour will agree with me that it was worthy of the trooping of the Colour by any of the Regiments in His Majesty's Brigade of Guards on the Horse Guards Parade in London, and I should like to take this opportunity of saying how proud I was to have been invited to take the salute at this parade.

A polo match followed after the special durbar. A reluctant Mountbatten was persuaded to play. A variety of polo dresses were kept ready for him, including a dozen tailors to alter/stitch a new dress if required. There were 136 ponies that were paraded for him to enable him to choose four for himself. Mountbatten could hardly extricate himself. Polo was followed by a movie in a new cinema hall inaugurated that very day. It belonged to one of the polo stick makers. Jai had given him that plot in 1933 after the famous and successful polo tour in England. The hall was appropriately named the 'Polo Victory'. They all watched an old film of the victorious polo team in action.

As part of the celebrations, Jai and Second Her Highness as well as Gayatri were weighed in silver, and the money distributed to the poor. This spectacular affair, accompanied by formal parades and informal festivities, went on for weeks.

Soon afterwards, Jai and Gayatri went to Cooch Behar for Bhaiya's Silver Jubilee. During this visit, Jai laid the foundation stone of an agriculture college in Cooch Behar (according to Gayatri, when Cooch Behar was merged with West Bengal, the work on this college was stopped).

The grand celebrations of the Silver Jubilee were followed by a grander celebration of the marriage of Mickey, Jai's eldest daughter by First Her Highness, with the Maharaj Kumar of Baria. Baria was a Rajput State in Gujarat. Mickey was 19. The groom was the nephew of Prithi Singh of Baria, who was one of the members of the famous polo team that 'devoured' England in 1933. It was to be the first marriage of a Jaipur princess in more than a century. It has been recorded in the Guinness Book as 'the most expensive wedding in the world'. The festivities lasted for two weeks. Jaipur, being an old household, was related to Rajput families all over the country and the princes had come from the length and breadth of India. Ram Bagh Palace was vacated again for the guests, and additional tents were put up in the gardens. The guest list was staggering, and prodigious effort was required for organizing the boarding, lodging and all logistics. The book of instructions giving out the details of coordination was two-inch thick. Menus for even the servants accompanying the guests, as also vantage points for the servants to see the celebrations from, were carefully worked out. Gayatri remembers that this was the only time she saw City Palace fully alive.

Gayatri was to select Mickey's trousseau. She did not have enough time to go to Delhi or Bombay; hence the mountain came to Mohammed. The best shops of Delhi and Bombay showed their choicest display in Jaipur. Gayatri selected 200 saris. Henry Cartier Bresson, a famous French photographer, came to take pictures. The wedding was the most splendid event to happen in Jaipur.

Soon after the wedding, Jai and Gayatri went off to England. This was Gayatri's first journey abroad since their marriage. She had not gone to London since 1938. While in England, Jai bought a house, built in 1820 in the late Georgian style, near East Grinsteat. It was called Saint Hill and built on a 400-acre farm.

From England, Jai and Gayatri went to the US (in that same year, i.e., 1938). This was the first time ever that either of them had visited the US. Jai was besieged with press reporters and photographers everywhere. Questions were frequently asked about the number of wives Jai had. This was also the first time that either of them had seen a skyscraper. Gayatri spoke of New York thus:

> That first night I hardly slept at all. I could not keep away from the windows from which I could see the city all lit up. I was enormously impressed by everything—the food, the shops, the cars, clothes people wore. And I was astonished at the efficiency of the telephone system and politeness of the operators.

Polo players being ubiquitous, Jai found many there. They visited Meadowbrook on Long Island to watch polo. Washington was the next stop, where they stayed with the Indian ambassador, Sir Benegal Rama Rau. They also visited Hollywood, meeting famous film stars, including Ronald Reagan, before returning to India.

Those halcyon days were followed by the most difficult period in Jai's life. These were the negotiations for the future. Nehru and Patel were giving repeated assurances that but for the three areas, defence, foreign affairs, and communications, the princely states would be left alone. Jaipur in any case had already travelled a considerable distance towards democratization. Even the Congress Movement in Jaipur had affirmed its loyalty to the maharaja. The people's faith in the maharaja was undiminished, and this fact would have been affirmed had a referendum taken place.

V.P. Menon never got tired of repeating that the principle of merger would not apply to the viable states, Jaipur being one of them. This was no surprise, for Jaipur had been in existence now for almost a 1000 years and was a vibrant state even before the Mughals invaded India. But the grind had begun, and the ratchet could not move in the opposite direction. Gayatri had a ringside view of the negotiation proceedings. She remarked, 'For Jai, of course, the merger of Jaipur into the Greater Rajasthan Union was politically wise and historically inevitable.' Factually, however, federation and merger had connotations that lay poles apart from one another. From the stance of non-applicability of the principle of merger to an ultimate merger, even of the viable states, was not a long journey. The uncertain future, the subtle political pressure, (the lack of confidence and cunning in the princes) along with a host of other imponderable factors, put the states of Rajputana into disarray. Nine small states in south-east Rajputana, headed by Kota (the place where Jai was studying before he was adopted as the successor of Madho Singh II), decided to merge their identity with the dominion.

Around the same time, four states in north-east Rajputana, Dholpur, Bharatpur, Karauli and Alwar (once a part of Jaipur), decided to merge and form the 'Matsya Union'.[6] Alwar and Bharatpur were the only two states in Rajputana where communal violence had occurred. Alwar was kept under house arrest in a hotel in Delhi. The threat of army intervention to maintain law and order loomed large over Bharatpur as well.

Jaipur, Jodhpur, Bikaner, and Jaisalmer were still holding out. Jinnah gave them a *carte blanche* and was prepared to accede to any terms that they might demand. But Menon and Patel's assurance and the presence of Mountbatten were more tempting and acceptable to Jaisalmer. The other three states (barring Jaisalmer) had also been classed as viable. There were many formal and informal meetings and confabulations on the telephone between Jaipur, Jodhpur, and Bikaner. The Maharaja of Bikaner was the oldest, whereas Maharaja Hanuwant Singh of Jodhpur was barely into his twenties.

Although Jai was younger to Bikaner, Jaipur was strategically and customarily a higher seat as well as being the more important of the two. Bikaner, in fact, is an offshoot of Jodhpur. Jai was the most agreeable among all and had the required political finesse. That notwithstanding, the three could never agree. Dr Karni Singh, the next ruler of Bikaner, in his book, *The Relations of the House of Bikaner with Central Powers 1465-1949*, is reticent about divulging why the three could not agree on a joint strategy saying: 'It would be indelicate to say why it did not happen.' Patel and Menon were at their devious best, tapping the telephones of the maharajas and making their moves accordingly. Jai's prime minister, Sir V.T. Krishnamachari, though a good administrator and a loyal subject, also had his sympathies for the dominion.

The next to fall was the mightiest of them all, the Maharana of Mewar. Udaipur was also one of the 18 viable states. However, this was a minor factor. Historically, Udaipur was a symbol of fierce independence and total defiance. The psychological blow of Udaipur's merger was telling. Jai was personally disturbed. Among his papers the following note was found:

Were there no men of cool common sense, who considered the main duty of state leadership to be the preservation of the states entrusted to their care?

Many of the rulers who talked big of fighting to the last did what weak characters always do when they should be acting up to it. Most of these rulers had seen themselves as Suns round which the whole of Hindustan revolved.

It did not occur to them for a moment that lakhs of their subjects had spent their whole lives without any guarantee of safety from them, and that they (the people) had taken the safety for granted as the main fulfilment owed to them. However, the rulers left reality behind, the reality of countless lives wrecked and unprotected, despite the people's unswerving loyalty to the ruler and unremitting toil in his service...

The constant game of cat and mouse put a great strain on the three. When the divide became clear, Jai briefly toyed with the idea of standing alone. Perhaps only for a fleeting moment because such a course would inevitably have had serious repercussions. The agony that Jai was undergoing can be fathomed from the letter Jai wrote to his eldest son, Bubbles, who would in the course of time, have taken over from Jai. Bubbles was not even 20 when Jai wrote:

> This letter is so different from the ones that I usually write and I know I have no business to worry you with these problems. I should leave you to your studies but all the decisions I take today will affect you and bind you down in the future and so I consider it my duty not only as your father but as the Ruler of this historic state, a heritage handed down from our renowned ancestors to which in turn we all dedicate our lives, to paint you a true picture of our position today.
>
> Our country is going through a revolutionary change and those of us who are going to be of any service to her must adapt ourselves to the changing circumstances. If we still persist in living on our laurels and in the way of life that existed 50 years ago we shall be asking for trouble and be wiped off the map.
>
> I shall now try to give you a clear picture of Rajputana as it is today. It breaks my heart to say so but I am afraid Rajputana is in the melting pot, and I see no bright future for her unless one of the rulers is prepared to make a sacrifice and take the lead. The picture of the states today is as follows...

After describing the sorry state of affairs prevalent in the other states of Rajputana at that time, Jai spoke about Jaipur:

> Jaipur, the state to which we all have the honour of belonging, stands out by itself. There is not a person today in India, who can

find a fault or point an accusing finger towards its ruler, administration or people.

This is the picture of Rajputana today, and now I come to the great decision I have to take, and that is whether to stand out and remain as we live today or whether to go to the help of Rajputana and form another Rajasthan and be their leader. If I become the leader of Rajputana, it will mean sacrificing the independence of Jaipur. On the other hand, no one can forecast how long any other state or we can remain independent because all the forces in the country are moving towards democratic ideals. So my dear boy, the sacrifice which seems so great today may prove in the end to be no sacrifice at all. Time and history will alone prove that.

According to the letter, Jai had consulted extensively with Mountbatten. The discussions went on throughout 1948, when Jai had another crash in November. Jai was to have gone to Delhi for negotiations with regard to the merger. Gayatri was to fly with him. However, Jai went a little early to the airport to check a plane that had been brought from America. The aircraft had two engines, though it could land and take off on only one. The pilots wanted to demonstrate the capability of the aircraft to Jai. The offer was too tempting, and Jai joined the pilot. Within a minute, the plane crashed. A horrified Gayatri, who was watching the entire scene from the airport along with Jai's pilot, rushed to the spot in a jeep and moved a bleeding and unconscious Jai away from the wreckage. This happened just in time. Within minutes the whole plane burst into flames, with a shattering explosion. Jai was taken to the hospital, and Gayatri headed for the Shila Devi Temple in Amber. It was a few weeks before Jai could be shifted to Ram Bagh.

The negotiations suffered a setback on account of Jai's accident. While he was still under treatment, the Indian National Congress had its Annual Session in Jaipur in 1948.[7]

Jawaharlal Nehru and Sarojini Naidu stayed at Ram Bagh with Jai.

On 11 January 1949, it was agreed that Jaipur, Jodhpur, Jaisalmer and Bikaner would merge into a union of greater Rajasthan, which would include the entire Rajputana. Jai was to be made the hereditary *Rajpramukh*. Menon had himself come down to give assurances on behalf of the Government of India. These included the following:

1. The rulers of Jaipur will be the hereditary *Rajpramukh* of Greater Rajasthan.
2. Jaipur will be the capital of Greater Rajasthan.
3. The ruler of Jaipur will have a privy purse of Rs 25 lakh.
4. No *Up-rajpramukh* will be appointed.

The Government of India reneged on these promises almost immediately. Even before the ink on the documents was dry, the Maharana of Udaipur was made the 'Maharaj *Pramukh*' for whatever it was worth and whatever it meant. The government also went back on the undertaking about hereditary succession. The *Rajpramukh*ship granted to Jai was truncated only for his own lifetime. The privy purse granted to him was juggled along with his allowances for the *Rajpramukh*, effectively reducing the amount from what had been promised. It may be worth noting that the Government of India received Rs 4,58,00,000 lakhs in cash, along with the other assets of the railways (in fact, an entirely functioning railway system along with the rolling stock) from Jaipur for a song. The State of Rajasthan got its assembly building and the Secretariat, from where the entire government functioned, as also the building which housed the state police headquarters. This was in addition to the various historic monuments like Amber Palace (excluding of course, the temple of Shila Devi which was a family deity), Hawa Mahal, Ranthambore Fort, Nahargarh Fort, observatories and the personal sanctuaries. The monetary value of what was handed over to the state government, at that time roughly worked out to Rs 15 crore in 1949. Similarly, cash and assets were given by the other states of Rajputana. Bikaner handed over Rs 8 crore in cash alone at the time of the merger.

Each of the assets handed over and the list of private properties to be retained by the maharaja were listed out specifically in a covenant that was signed between the maharaja and the central government. Jai too signed a similar document. This document included other privileges that the maharajas were to enjoy. In addition, it was provided that a public holiday would be observed on Jai's birthday, within the Jaipur division of Greater Rajasthan.

Jaipur State's forces also merged with the Indian Army. There was some solace that Sawai Man Guards, which is now the 17th battalion of the Rajputana Rifles retains the name of Sawai Man in its title. The Jaipur Cavalry was converted to 61st Cavalry, which was stationed at Jaipur and has continued here till date.

Patel and Menon arrived on 30 March 1949 to inaugurate the new state of Greater Rajasthan, and administer the oath of office to Jai as the *Rajpramukh* of Rajputana. The function was organized in City Palace.

An era had effectively come to an end.

---

1   Wife of Col. Govind Singh (popularly known as Gomji) of Khatipura. Gomji was ADC and later MA to Jai. He commanded the Old Kachhwaha Horse, 61st Cavalry.

2   The Chamber of Princes had been constituted in February 1921 and comprised the rulers of various Indian kingdoms. The aim was to meet annually and discuss subjects of mutual interest in the rapidly changing political environment. Despite its ostensible gloss, it proved to be a damp squib.

3   New Delhi had initially said that the viable states would not be touched. A list of 18 viable states was drawn up after a detailed study; Jaipur was one of them. The government stance then gradually veered.

4   It may be noted that Sir Mirza Ismail and Sir V.T. Krishnamachari were two of the five individuals most sought after by the progressive princely states for the job of prime minister. That Jai managed to get two of them, one after the other, speaks of his involvement, devotion, and dedication to his state. The other three were Sardar K.M. Panikkar, Sir Manubhai Mehta, and C.S. Venkatachari.

4   *Qaimkhanis* are Rajputs who converted to Islam.

6   The present territory of the State of Rajasthan was known as 'Matsya Desh' in ancient times. It is referred to as the kingdom of Raja Virat in the epic, Mahabharata.

7   That the Congress decided to hold its first Annual Session in Independent India in Jaipur speaks of the rapport of Jai's government with the Praja Mandal (a limb of the Congress) as also the distance Jaipur had already travelled on the road to democracy. In fact, Pandit Heera Lal Shastri, the first chief minister of Rajasthan, had stated in one of the Constitutional Reform Committee meetings in 1942: 'I stand for the establishment of full responsible government under the aegis of His Highness the Maharaja, and to this end in view, the Constitutional Reforms Committee should proceed to frame a constitution for Jaipur. The people of Jaipur should have the fullest freedom to carry on His Highness's Government and His Highness should occupy the exalted position of a constitutional ruler far above party politics. Jaipur should enjoy full responsible government as an integral part of a free and independent India.'

LIFE IN FREE INDIA

The British were called the 'co-architects' of India at the dawn of freedom. However, what happened to the princes is a poignant tale of total deceit in the name of democracy. The lofty ideals of people's power, equality, and verbal tactics were employed to go back on every single promise made. In the temple of Galta, there used to be an idol of the deity Narsingh. According to legend, the state of Jaipur was to last as long as the idol was there. Soon after Jai signed the documents of merger, the idol vanished and with it disappeared the hope of an independent Jaipur.

Jai had the sterling quality of letting go of the past. Hence, on taking over as *Rajpramukh* he immersed himself in his new task with enthusiasm. Unfortunately, the title was merely ceremonial. The common people never realized that power had been lost. Wherever he went, people accosted him with their problems, big or small. Jai had to explain to all of them that he was no longer in power. But Jai's popularity was still huge, and it was a constant source of irritation for politicians. During every function, whether formal, informal or political, every single person of any stature was neglected, and Jai invariably received all the attention and adulation. The Maharaja of Kota had been appointed *Up-rajpramukh* (contrary to the promise made) and the Maharana of Udaipur, the Maharaj *pramukh*. Udaipur was to have taken precedence over Jai in all formal functions. However, such formal functions were as fictitious as the appointments.

The parade held to disband the Rajputana State Forces (including the Jaipur State Forces) was one of the first functions Jai attended. It was an irony of sorts. Jai was very proud of the forces he had raised along the lines of the British forces. A magnificent parade was held in front of the building that Jai had had built as barracks for the troops (where the present Government of the State of Rajasthan sits). Jai took the salute on this historical occasion. Gayatri records:

> All of us, the spectators, could feel the tears pricking behind our eyes, but Jai, looking proud and sombre, gazed out at the perfect performance of his men, saluted the colours, and accepted them as the various officers handed them to him. Only Jai's favourite regiment, the Sawai Man Guards, which he had raised himself, retained their identity when they were incorporated into the Indian Army. They are still known as the 17th Rajputana Rifles (Sawai Man Guard). All the other Jaipur cavalry regiments and some of the other States Forces cavalry were amalgamated into the 61st Cavalry, now the only cavalry regiment left in India.

Jai's 38th birthday was celebrated on 22 August 1949. A note scribbled by him, immediately after ceasing to be king, reveals the real Jai and his feelings. The note is quoted in full below:

> I am writing an account of my birthday under the new changes as this was the first occasion after the formation of Greater Rajasthan. I feel happy and proud that I find no change in my people's love, affection and loyalty towards me, and I had a rousing reception from

all sects of my people wherever I went and met them at most functions.

I was greeted at sunrise with the booming of guns from Nahargarh, and a kiss from my beautiful wife which made a perfect beginning. I then had a swim after which all the personal servants came and did their *nazars* to me, which I touched and did not take. Then I changed into an *achkan* and *safa* to go to City Palace for the puja and other ceremonies.

The route most of the way was thronged by the people and as I passed them I was greeted with shouts of 'Maharaja Man Singh*ji ki Jai'*, to which I responded by waving to the people.

At 11 a.m., I did puja at the haveli and then went and did the *walbati* at Shri Govind Dev*ji's* temple. The gardens were thronged with townspeople who gave greater welcome than ever till I came back to Chandra Mahal.

Then I went and did 'Baras pujan' in Shereth Niwas doing *bhati* to Guruji on the way.

Then I held a durbar in Sarbata of rather an unusual type from the ones we use to have on birthday occasions. I only invited 'Tazimi and Khas Chofti sardars and their eldest sons. This was well attended and all the sardars turned out in red and gold and we had a collection of about 90 sardars and sons. After the *nazars* were over, I sat down and called the sardars close to me so that I could talk to them.

In few chosen words that came from my happy heart, I told them that I have never been happier than having so many of them in the durbar. And that with all the changes in Rajputana States, I was proud that Jaipur was like before and this was owing to their loyalty and affection for me. I wanted to adopt some changes, but not without their wishes. For this I proposed a Council, under Maharawal of Samode, to make suggestions (regarding) what customs we might keep and what we could do away with. I also told them that we are one family and that it rests on one another to hold our prestige and honour in the new changes. I assured them on my side that I shall always look after their interest and prayed to Mataji that she will always guide us all and save us from doing any deed or action which would put disgrace or shame on the Kachhwaha family or the Jaipur State.

We then dispersed from the durbar and they all came and had drinks with me in Chandra Mahal.

I then freely mixed with them and talked to them and was greatly touched with their expressions and sentiments of loyalty and devotion to me and my family. We then dispersed for lunch. I had a quiet lunch with the family, which was attended by both my wives and Isarda Bhabi.

I then had some rest till I went to the garden party to which all those who usually come to the durbar were invited.

Before going to the garden party, I had a request from the old officials of the Jaipur State that they would like to present *nazars* to me so I asked them to come before the garden party. I received them in Sarbata. They all came and presented their *nazar* in the usual manner, but in their case I only touched it and did not take it, which created quite a surprise to some of the officials. I then gave them a short talk and said: 'Gentlemen, I am greatly touched by the display of loyalty and affection shown by you all on this occasion and assure you that whatever change may take place my love and care of you all in no way will be affected as Jaipur-ians.' (All the officials were greatly moved by my words.)

I then went to the party held in City Palace garden, and it was well attended by all people, officials and politicians. I spent about half an hour going round the people and talking to them and then left the party after the band had played the Jaipur Anthem.

I then changed and bathed and then went to the Zenana Majils in 'Bada Rawala', which was as usual full of screaming women and children, but they all gave me a happy smile and after taking *nazar* of the ladies I came away.

The army officers had also requested that they all wanted to present *nazar* so I had arranged to see them all at a special party 'cocktails' after the Zenana Majils. So now, I went to see all the officers of the Rajasthan Army, who had collected in City Palace garden. They were all linked up and after I had taken my place on the Silver Chair they all came one by one and presented their *nazars*, which I took standing up and kept. Then all the retired officers also did the *nazar*, but my surprise had no limit when the Indian Army officers came forward and did *nazar*. I took their *nazar* and kept it, as I did not want to make a difference between the two by which their feeling might be affected.

I then asked all the officers to come round me and in few chosen words said:

'Brother officers you have greatly touched my heart by the display of love and loyalty shown to me by this gesture of yours this evening and presenting *nazars,* and that happiness is still greater since today the feelings of State and Indian officers is equal for me. There is no reason for the two forces to feel different in any way for today we all stand for one cause and that is to serve our country to the best of our ability. I want to assure all those under my command that I consider my first and foremost duty to serve them and watch their and their family interest at all times. Words fail me to express my feeling adequately this evening but you will understand my feeling better than I can ever put them in words. I hope you will all join me in having a glass of champagne and *asha* [a local brew].'

We had a happy party, in fact, one of the best I have ever had with the Army boys. We were all in a happy mood. The party was so good that it lasted from 8 p.m. to 11 p.m., and they [Army boys] all [so] carried me away by feelings difficult to express that I forgot my dinner engagement. I left the party at 11 p.m. with fond farewells. I am proud to have this fine lot of men under my command and am confident that the spirit that was displayed on this occasion makes me believe that no task is insurmountable for us [sic].

I came back to Ram Bagh for dinner where we were having a family party composed of relatives and members of staff and their families. After good drink and good food, in a hilarious mood, I said goodnight to all and went to bed.

This was my first birthday as Rajpramukh of Greater Rajasthan, and I can confidently say that it was just as happy and gay as the ones I had as Ruler of Jaipur and the display of love, loyalty and devotion shown by all the people greatly touched my heart.

I pray to Mataji that she will always guide me and bless me so that I will serve the people well and that the whole of Rajasthan will love me and trust me. I could not have wished for a happier birthday.

Even Gayatri was moved by the spontaneous response of the people. In *A Princess Remembers*, she says:

> In fact, election aside, I do not think I have ever witnessed in Jaipur a more impressive and spontaneous demonstration of loyalty and warmth than on Jai's first birthday after the merger of the state. The people behaved exactly as if Jai were still their ruler, cheering him repeatedly whenever he appeared in public, showering him with messages of goodwill. Very possibly it was indications such as these that led to an increase of caution and distrust in the government's attitude towards the princes over the next few years.

Having taken over new responsibilities, Jai could not afford the luxury of going abroad. Jai and Gayatri escaped to Kashmir for a fortnight during the summers. Early in October, Gayatri went off to Bombay and joined Ma. Jagat was born here, two weeks premature.[1] A public holiday was declared in Jaipur city and gun salute was fired from the Nahargarh fort. The chief minister and all the dignitaries went to Ram Bagh to congratulate Jai. The ADC who barged into Jai's room to give him the news of Jagat's birth was presented with a new car. Five years later, Jai's elder brother from Isarda, Bahadur Singh, who had no son of his own, adopted Jagat.

For the next two years, polo was resumed. Jai had a handicap of nine before the war; it was now five. He was underrated at this handicap. Huge crowds thronged to the Ram Bagh polo club whenever Jai played in any tournament. The Argentine team came to India in 1950 and visited Delhi, Bombay, and Jaipur. Jai's team had won the Indian Championship Cup in Argentina for seven years in succession. Polo became popular again. The Indian Polo Association was formed, and Jai was made the president. Subsequently Jai visited England again, where Prince Philip gave special attention to the game after his return from Malta.

Jai bought a flat in Grosvenor Square in London. Since all his three sons, Bubbles, Joey, and Pat, were going to Harrow, one after the other, England became, as Gayatri called it, 'our second home'.

While politicians were desperately attempting to make inroads into Jai's powers and popularity, the VVIPs, be they Indian or foreign, would deem their visit to Jaipur incomplete without being Jai's guests. Lord and Lady Mountbatten were one of the first ones to visit Jai. Jai had first met Lady Mountbatten way back in 1921, when he was at Mayo College. (As a boy, he was standing in for his ailing adoptive father.) During their second visit, Lady Mountbatten also visited the girl's school started by Gayatri in Jaipur. Miss Lutter, the first principal, who had taught in Burma before taking over the school, was worried about one of her ex-students in Burma and mentioned this to Lady Mountbatten. She received a response from her within a week. Dr Rajendra Prasad, the first president of India, Chakravarty Rajagopalachari, the first Indian governor general, Dr Ambedkar, the architect of the Indian Constitution, and Jawaharlal Nehru accompanied by Indira Gandhi, all enjoyed Jai's hospitality. In fact, Dr Ambedkar recollected with gratitude his indebtedness to Gayatri's Baroda grandfather, who had financed a penniless Ambedkar's education as a child. Among the foreign dignitaries were Mrs Eleanor Roosevelt (who visited on the festival of Holi), Bulganin and Khrushchev.

The duplicity of the politicians came to the fore during the first general elections in India in 1952. Pandit Heera Lal Shastri, Jai's teacher at Mayo, an old acquaintance and a prominent Congress leader, came to consult Jai. Jai had to politely remind him that being the *Rajpramukh*, he could not opine on the internal matters of a political party. But there is no doubt that had Jai been unshackled and had he contested the elections, he would have routed the political parties as the young Maharaja of Jodhpur, Jaswant Singh, had done.

Jaswant Singh was, incidentally, the first cousin of Second Her Highness. He contested as an independent. His opponent, Jai Narain Vyas, a prominent leader who subsequently became the chief minister of Rajasthan, forfeited his deposit. The candidates Jaswant Singh had supported won by a handsome majority. Unfortunately, Jaswant Singh died in an air crash two days before the declaration of the results, unaware of what a magnificent performance he had given. Out of 35 of his candidates, 31 had won—an indication of the popularity of the maharajas at that time. Needless to add, had Jai been permitted to contest and participate similarly, along with Udaipur and Kota, the history of Rajputana would have been different. However, all the three were strapped in sinecures.

The politicians cunningly kept the maharajas on their toes. They hung a Damocles' sword over their heads, threatening them with curtailment or suspension of their privy purses if they indulged in politics. This was euphemistically termed 'activities against the interest of the state'. Practically, it applied only to the princes who were not candidates of the ruling party. This clause was not applicable to princes who were part of the ruling elite, like the Maharani of Gwalior. Some, like Jai, had the solace of a *Rajpramukh-ship* hobbling their independence. Kota and Udaipur were similarly controlled. Thus, the popular maharajas were effectively removed from the scene.

The political minions had been doing their job of making life difficult for the maharajas on every conceivable occasion.

The higher echelons commenced their part in 1955 in a polished manner, chipping away at the covenant, which had been inscribed as sacrosanct in the Constitution. It started with a polite letter from Nehru that made fleeting observations regarding the 'anachronism' of the privy purses and the lifetime appointment of *Rajpramukhs*. These were allegedly 'out of keeping with the directive principles of our Constitution (and as unjustifiable to our people)... the payment of large sums of money from public funds to the princes many of whom discharge no function at all.' No one reminded the Centre that the amount of cash received by the Government of India from the Jaipur Treasury would have been sufficient to meet the requirement of the privy purse on an interest of 0.25 per cent. The directive principles were as clearly defined when Menon and Patel were bending backwards to get the maharajas to sign the document to join the dominion. But politics is the art of the possible. The princes were taught to stay above politics and not sully their hands by joining the fight. Politicians, on the other hand, would cease to exist unless they could be champions of the cesspool. The unwary princes were easily gobbled up in this unequal fight.

Nehru's letters were polite, but their purport was conspicuously clear. However, V.P. Menon, who was the man involved in the nitty-gritty of the merger, commented on the 'Integration of the Indian States'. He refuted the allegation that the price paid for integration in the shape of the privy purses was too high. He spoke about the government getting a railway system of 12,000 miles and an immense cash balance of Rs 77 crore that excluded buildings, palaces, and other infrastructure. Till recently, the Rajasthan Government's Assembly, the police headquarters and other offices, functioned from buildings inherited from the maharaja. The secretariat is still housed in one of these buildings today. Menon held that 'if these are weighed against the total amount of privy purses, the latter would seem insignificant.' As it is, the privy purses were diminishing with each successor's death, and the total amount paid in the form of privy purses was merely 15 per cent of the cash inherited by the Union. However, now that the deed was done, the parties had become much too unequal in their bargaining power.

Although, there was much fretting and fuming among the princes, what had been set in motion could no longer be stopped. Nehru and Jai exchanged letters frequently, and both were temperate in their tone. Jai pleaded with Nehru that what was granted to the princes in exchange of surrendering their 'ancient heritage with one bold stroke of pen' had been guaranteed in the Constitution. Jai urged Nehru 'to emulate advanced democracies like England and USA where even minor amendments are made with meticulous care and serious thought'. The government's strategy was to move at a leisurely pace, picking up the subject and leaving it for a later date. The sword could not have been more frighteningly placed. Gobind Ballabh Pant, the home minister, also made polite suggestions about princes contributing 15 per cent of their privy purses as government loans. Jai was indignant though polite. He wrote: 'The princes are not the only people in India, there are others who could be asked to contribute, such as the zamindars and landowners who received compensation and also business magnates.'

However, the politicians had forgotten the desperation with which they sought cooperation from the princes. Jai did suggest to Nehru that the former rulers were unhappy and thought that the worst had already happened to them. This was a dangerous state of affairs. He, therefore, suggested that the services of the ex-rulers be utilized by associating them with the local or central government. They would then feel of some use to the country. Mountbatten, in his speech delivered to 'the world's most exclusive fraternity', had begged them to 'marry the new India' because the princes had the skills India would need. They could offer their services to the nation and find a new role for themselves. Tragically, the 'role', what little was assigned, was also being shrunk. The skills, what little they had, were going a-begging.

The princely states had covered about 48 per cent of the area of the Indian Dominion before 1947. The population of this area formed 28 per cent of the total population of the dominion. The privy purses were fixed for the rulers with due regard to their income before integration, with a ceiling of Rs 10 lakh. Eleven rulers were to be paid more. The privy purses totalled Rs 5.8 crore. The Ministry of States issued a memorandum of privileges in 1949, which contained an itemized list of 34 privileges. At the time of the merger, the princes were described as 'imbued with imagination, foresight and patriotism and as co-architects of a democratic' and united India. Sardar Vallabhbhai Patel, minister in the newly formed Ministry of States, made a speech on 12 October 1949 in the Constituent Assembly. He pointed out that the Madhya Bharat *Rajpramukh* alone gave sufficient cash assets which, if invested, would cover payments to the rulers as privy purses, and that payments to the rulers represented one-fourth of what they were previously enjoying. He said that there was nothing by which the rulers could be forced to merge their states with India, and that the privy purses were a *quid pro quo* with the rulers for parting with their ruling powers and the dissolution of their states. He regarded this as a small price for the bloodless revolution and avoidance of mischief. He exhorted the Constituent Assembly that the Indian people, on their part, should ensure fully the guarantee given to them and concluded: 'Our failure to do so would be a breach of faith and seriously prejudice the stabilization of the New Order.'

V.P. Menon (who was Secretary to the Ministry) reiterated the sentiments in his book, *The Story of the Integration of the Indian States*. He catalogued the number of villages, palaces, museums, buildings, stables, garages, fleets of motorcars, and aeroplanes surrendered by the rulers. According to him, 'The price paid as privy purses was not too high for integration and, indeed, it was insignificant when compared with what the rulers had lost.' Lofty words. Time took the loftiness away, and the princes became incompatible with an egalitarian social order. The constitutional guarantees were whittled down considerably.

The *coup de grace* was delivered in October 1956, when Jai received three letters, one from President Dr Rajendra Prasad, another from Prime Minister Nehru and yet another from Home Minister Gobind Ballabh Pant. All three had only one message: Jai would no longer be *Rajpramukh* from 31 October 1956. It was a bolt from the blue. Nehru's letter was not only didactic and prosaic, it was most unconvincing. He wrote:

> It is fitting that, as India advances towards her goal of a Socialist State, a greater degree of uniformity and equality should prevail in the country. The highest privilege that any of us in this country can have is that of a citizen of India with equal rights and obligations with others.
>
> Whatever office we may hold or whether we hold an office or not, those privileges and obligations continue. I have no doubt that

you will continue to take deep interest in the progress of the country and, more especially, in the welfare of the people of the State... I feel sure we will have the benefit of your guidance and cooperation.

This was one act of state that was neither grounded in law nor did it pretend to be so. It was an unpropitious change constituting a new and unwholesome departure. As Chief Justice of India, M. Hidayatullah was to observe later in the case of Madhav Rao Scindia v/s the Union of India, 'a state cannot act "catastrophically" outside the ordinary law.' Justice G.K. Mitter, in his minority judgment, said, 'When they accepted the constitution,[2] the rulers never imagined that they would be playthings of the Executive Government of the Union of India, to be thrown out like pawns off the chequer board of politics at any moment when the government felt their pressure was irksome or that they were anachronistic in the democratic set up of India.'

Jai had always conducted himself gracefully and sincerely. He was instrumental in getting the recalcitrant thakurs to veer around to the new order. He was deeply hurt as he was neither consulted nor warned about the sudden change. He replied to the prime minister:

My dear Prime Minister,

I am writing to express my deep sense of gratitude to you for the kind terms you referred to me in your letter of 4 October and for the appreciation of my services as Rajpramukh by the Government of India.

I hope I shall not be misunderstood when I say that I feel hurt at the manner in which my services are being terminated after all the assurances which had been given to me by persons in authority on behalf of the Government of India and provision made in the

Constitution of our country, all of which I regarded fondly as sacrosanct and which had given me a sense of security. I now find it most distressing that in spite of sincere co-operation and unflinching loyalty on my part throughout the last seven years my official connections with the administration should cease so abruptly.

I would, however, like to take this opportunity of assuring you that wherever I may be placed I shall, in future as in the past, continue to devote myself to the service of our country, and in particular to take deep interest in my home state of Rajasthan with which I and my family have had the closest ties for hundreds of years.

With kind regards,

Yours sincerely
Man Singh

Nehru was less than diplomatic in his reply and questioned whether the 'Constitution should be petrified'. In the same letter, Nehru dilated on the economic situation (probably a precursor to the abolition of the privy purses). It was, as Crewe says, 'another notch on the irreversible ratchet system'. As Dhananajaya Singh says in *The House of Marwar* '... And frightening indeed is the realization that the foundations of the world's largest democracy rest on the rubble of broken promises, cemented with a mixture of wilful deceit and authoritarianism.' But this was not the end of it. More was to come. There were unforeseen minor hiccups in Jai's family. His son Jagat, a little boy then, came home upset because his friends had told him that his father was no longer the most important man in Jaipur.

For the first time in his adult life, Jai was truly and completely unemployed.

Jai, as a matter of habit, never grieved over spilt milk. The times were frustrating, and Jai sought solace in polo. He was the president of the Indian Polo Association. The association had been invited for the international matches to be held in the summer of 1957 in England. So far, polo teams from various princely states used to go abroad. This was the first time that a team selected at the national level represented the country. While the best of the ponies were available in India, these had to be left home because the Suez Canal was closed and it was impossible for the well-cared, trained ponies to undertake an arduous journey around Africa. Jai thus, had to look for mounts (ponies) in England itself.

The second general elections were held in India in 1957. Jai wrote a confidential letter to Nehru, asking for 'your guidance about my standing for Parliament at the request of the Jaipur people'. Jai went to the extent of stating: '...things have moved so fast that I have been swept off my feet and I had to inadvertently commit myself to a certain extent to the people...' and further that, '...whatever responsibilities are thrust upon me by the public, I shall hope I shall have your blessings.' Nehru was puzzled and did not give any positive or encouraging response. He simply referred the letter to the election committee and replied in a non-committal manner. That was the end of the matter.

However, the Chief Minister of Rajasthan approached Gayatri and asked her to consider standing as a Congress Party candidate from Jaipur. The reason why the chief minister decided to request Gayatri and not Jai must lie in the realm of conjecture. Gayatri rushed to Jai for guidance. He told her she 'might be able to do something useful for Jaipur, if she joined the Congress Party'. Gayatri was not enthused with the idea. The corruption in the Congress was too conspicuous and Jai had, in fact, written a letter to Nehru expressing his anguish at the state of affairs. Besides, the Congress had spared no punches for the princes. 'Princes bashing' was an indispensable appendage to the 'socialist image'. Gayatri held that it would be dishonest to represent a party that had forsaken the ideals of Gandhi.

One thing was, however, clear from the enthusiastic response of the inner circle of advisors. Gayatri would have to take the plunge. The only questions were the timing and more importantly, the party she would choose. The news of Gayatri's impending arrival on the political scene could not be kept a secret. Unsolicited advice gushed in. Much sentiment flowed against the Congress. Gayatri, therefore, politely declined to represent the Congress and went off to England with the Indian Polo Team, which did not have a very triumphant tour. Except for winning the gold cup at Deauville with old team-mates Rao Raja Hanut Singh, the Maharaja of Idar, and Bijay Singh, son of Rao Raja Hanut Singh, there was nothing much to write home about.

On their return, Jai and Gayatri were horrified to see old buildings of archaeological importance being demolished, and encroachments coming up in the old city. Jai had expressly forbidden new constructions in the walled city. The walls of the old city were entirely demolished. Gayatri immediately wrote to Nehru, who replied promptly, saying: 'It is a sacrilege what they are doing to Jaipur. I am writing to the chief minister that this work should be stopped immediately.' Nehru did write. The demolitions did stop, but passive negligence of the monuments began. Unguided, unprincipled, and undisciplined democracy is never receptive to ideas that do not reap immediate returns.

This was probably the first though not the last time that Jai realized his helplessness. Ever a man with foresight, Jai first decided to reduce his expenditure. Their private plane was given up much to the chagrin of Gayatri, who had enjoyed the use of this one right from the age of 21. Jai then set up various trusts to provide for his children and to save the heritage of Jaipur City. It was at this time that work was begun in earnest for the establishment of the famous Museum Trust in City Palace. Unfortunately, Jai's initial choice of persons to manage it was poor and the Museum Trust had more than its fair share of teething troubles.

Jai was a progressive thinker beyond doubt, and much ahead of the other princes in recognizing the gravity of the new situation. Bubbles, having studied at Harrow, joined the Army in 1951. Joey did a brief spell with the Rothschild's bank in London and shifted to Calcutta for work. Pat was already in the tea business. At this time, the other princes considered work to be below their dignity.

It was decided that Ram Bagh Palace would be converted into a hotel. This idea came to Gayatri and Bubbles during the Delhi polo season, when they overheard the Oberois talking about the 'cataclysmic project', as Gayatri called it. Everyone in the family was naturally very upset at the thought of leaving Ram Bagh.

Gayatri and Jai were on their way to England for the summer of 1958. Jagat, then nine, was with Second Her Highness. She died a day after Jai and Gayatri left Jaipur. Bubbles was an adjutant in the President's Body Guard in Delhi at that time. He traced Jai at the airport and informed him about the death of Second Her Highness. She was 42 when she died.

Jai, Gayatri, and Bubbles drove back to Jaipur for the funeral. Thereafter, Jai decided to shift to what was earlier a

British Residency[3] and had, subsequently, been converted to a guesthouse at the time of Micky's wedding. It was re-named Rajmahal. The place was remodelled to suit the needs of Jai and Gayatri. Finally, when the family moved to Rajmahal, it was only Jai, Gayatri and Jagat. Gayatri could not easily reconcile to her old home (Ram Bagh) being accessible to strangers who were able to afford it. In her words, 'Jai used to complain, half amused and half irritated, that I used to treat hotel guests as interlopers.'

Soon, there were changes made in City Palace also. Jai started the City Palace Museum, now more popularly known as the Sawai Man Singh II Trust Museum. The museum has various sections. There are priceless manuscripts in the *Pothikhana*, some of them dating back to the 12th century, which are nonpareil in calligraphy as well as painting. The art gallery has on display miniatures from the Deccan and Malwa Schools and the works of celebrated artists of the 18th century. Astronomical works in Latin, Arabic, Persian and Sanskrit (collected by Sawai Jai Singh II) also form part of the museum. An old copy of *Ain-e-Akbari,* along with its Hindi translation by Gomani Ram Kayasth, is one of the priceless books kept here. The translation was done on the directions of Sawai Pratap Singh in 1775. Carpets brought by Mirza Raja Jai Singh from Herat, Lahore, and Agra are also on display. Besides other art objects, the *Silehkhana* stores the various weapons that were used as well as seized during the Mughal period. Textiles and costumes are displayed in a separate section housed in the upper stories of Mubarak Mahal where our can also see exquisitely woven and embroidered clothes in silk and gold lace.

Jai took a keen interest in the museum. During the 1965 Indo-Pak war, apprehending a danger to some of the exclusive items due to bombardment, Jai took the *Razm-Namh* and the *Shahi Ramayan* out of the museum and kept them with him.

There had been no addition to the zenana after the death of Madho Singh II. Consequent to his marriage with Gayatri, Jai's family life was like any other ordinary family, with husband, wife and their son Jagat, living as one unit. Consequently, the strength of the zenana in City Palace, which was 500 when Gayatri arrived in 1940, dwindled. When the museum became functional, the rest of the people from the zenana were also employed there or given land and sent home. Now, the only sounds that could be heard in City Palace were those of the tourists visiting the museum.

Jai constantly endeavoured to live with changed times, trying to salvage what little prestige was left to him in his private capacity and balancing it with apprehensions for the future of his children.

Jai continued to observe the traditions of Jaipur as he had inherited them. There was, for instance, a custom to visit the temple of Shila Devi in Amber, after recovering from a bout of measles, chicken pox, or small pox, for the purpose of thanksgiving. Jai, after one such bout, went for the thanksgiving, driving his own car. The crowd recognized him, and he received a tumultuous welcome. This kind of spontaneous expression of love and affection was the only thing left that sustained Jai and Gayatri. There was little else to assuage their feelings. Since Jai had ceased to be the *Rajpramukh*, he was no longer deluged with invitations to attend official functions. As mentioned earlier, Jai's immense popularity with the public was a constraint and a cause of heartburn among the 'popular' politicians. At any function or inauguration where a minister or an important dignitary was the chief guest, and if Jai happened to be present, the heartiest and loudest applause was reserved for Jai. It was invariably at the cost of the VIPs. Even the polo matches were as popular, and Jai used to be mobbed whenever he appeared in public.

Jai had been offered the ambassadorship of Argentina, but he had politely declined since he did not want to go so far away from the state. His exasperation on the state of affairs was conspicuous and yet quiet in its dignity and restraint.

It was during this time that Chakravarty Rajagopalachari, a Tamil Brahmin more popularly known as Rajaji, broke away from the Congress because of his differences with the parent organization and formed a new party, the Swatantra (Independent) Party, which Gayatri decided to join. She took the consent of a sleepy Jai, early in the morning, on the day of Pat's engagement. As it turned out, it was an inappropriate time for a political baptism, since the Queen of England was to arrive in Delhi soon on an official visit. Jaipur was on the itinerary.

Jai's son Pat got engaged to the daughter of Ila, Gayatri's sister who had secretly married the Maharaja of Tripura. The nobles of Jaipur attended this ceremony in traditional regalia and brought alive the memories of yore.

The Queen of England visited India in 1961. Jai had met her at a polo game in Windsor and requested her to visit Jaipur. The queen consented, and Jai immediately contacted Mrs Vijaylaxmi Pandit, the Indian High Commissioner in England, and Sir Michale Adeane, the Private Secretary to the queen to arrange her visit. The queen was expected in Jaipur on 23 January. Political heavyweights in Delhi and Jaipur found this impending visit unpalatable. A sports league in Britain made protests about the tiger shoot that was being organized for the queen.[4] The headlines of the newspapers screamed. Nehru wrote to Jai asking whether live bait would be used during shikar. Jai incidentally, had never used live bait ever and even earlier, shikars used to be organized with the help of the haka party. Nehru was satisfied on this account but promptly wrote another letter again based on newspaper reports about the queen's reception at Jaipur. Nehru wrote: 'I see in *The Statesman* today something about a durbar being held in Jaipur. I do not know what it is, and perhaps the description is exaggerated. Anyhow, it will not be proper to hold anything in the nature of a durbar or to call it as such. I have already received objections to it...'

Jai assured Nehru again that he was not so irresponsible. Nehru was informed that it was a reception and not a durbar and that at all such receptions, including the one held for Pat's engagement, the events were organized in a particular manner with the nobles dressed in their regalia. There was no reason for anybody's sensibilities to be offended, since traditional customs were being followed.

A few days before the queen's visit, Jai had gone to inspect a parade, when a horse swished its tail and wounded Jai's eye. Jai rushed to the hospital and told the ophthalmologist, 'I don't mind if you have to remove my eye after her visit, but I must be all right for the queen.' As it turned out, Jai recovered in time and later sent a large quantity of corneal grafts from London to the doctor as a gift of gratitude.

The queen's visit was a huge success. After receiving her, Jai, along with the queen, drove down to City Palace in an open car, followed by Prince Philip and Bubbles. On their arrival at the City Palace entrance, they were transported on an elephant. Gayatri received the queen in the Audience Pavilion.

The governor sent a negative report of the entire event to the government. He first said that Jai had only invited the chief minister and the minister for public works, who was one of the maharajas of a smaller state, for the reception. He also complained that instructions had been sent for everybody to come in turbans. The chief minister, out of pique, threatened that he would come in a Gandhi cap. The instructions about turbans were allegedly withdrawn and all the ministers were invited. As it turned out, all of them came wearing turbans. However, the governor grumbled that they were not introduced to the queen, who was seated in a separate box. He also alleged that tickets were sold for the people to watch the event, and the money had to be refunded after the government intervened. Such baseless canards were indicative of the rancour as well as the vacillation in political thinking. The reception at City Palace was a private event, but the politicians wanted to be invited. And even as guests, they wanted to influence, direct and decide the manner and sequence of events.

There was a formal dinner in the evening at Rajmahal, after which a special train took the royal couple to the shooting lodge at Sawai Madhopur. Col. Kesari Singh had made elaborate arrangements for the shoot. The luxurious train had a telephone in each compartment and was well-equipped for the shoot. Since it was a private trip, even the ADCs were not taken. Jai's four sons, of course, formed part of the entourage.

The Duke of Edinburgh shot a tiger on the first day. A picnic lunch was organized thereafter. The next day, after the shoot, a visit to the fort at Ranthambhore was followed by a dinner at the shooting lodge. The guests were treated to Colonel Kesari's anecdotes. All in all, the visit could not have been more satisfying for Jai and Gayatri and more dissatisfying for the politicians.

Gayatri topped it up by publicly announcing her decision to join the Swatantra Party immediately after the visit. This enraged the ruling party. The chief minister (forgetting his earlier invitation to Gayatri to contest on the ruling party ticket) announced in the State Assembly that princes joining party politics would stand to forfeit privy purses. Sir V.T. Krishnamachari, who had been Jai's prime minister, was now a well-placed government official. He wrote to Jai about the undesirability of Gayatri's plans.

This was the first time the Kachhwahas were opposing Delhi in almost a 1000 years. It will always remain a moot point as to what would have happened had Gayatri decided to be part of the Delhi government, more particularly, in view of the fact that Jaipur was a leading house, and that a lot of smaller principalities would have followed Jaipur for the asking. In those days, the ruling party was on a speedy downslide. The people were longing for the more peaceful days of the maharajas. Jai had initially wanted Gayatri to join the Congress, suggesting she might be able to stem the rot more effectively from within. However, Gayatri differed. Had she agreed to the suggestion, the history of Rajputana would have been markedly different. Jai, who had fallen in love with Gayatri because of her strong and independent streak, on a point of principle, never trampled on her convictions. In fact, on almost all points where there could have been a disagreement, Jai adopted a rather laid back attitude and permitted Gayatri her own counsel. This time too, Gayatri politely brushed aside Jai's suggestion.

During summer, Jai and Gayatri went to England. Mountbatten considered Gayatri's joining the Swatantra Party 'thoughtless'. During this sojourn, Jai kept himself busy with polo and Gayatri settled into the new house near Ascot, which was smaller than Saint Hill. Jagat was moved from Mayo and enrolled at Ludgrove Preparatory School, close to their new house.

On their return, Gayatri found an invitation from the Swatantra Party to contest for the Jaipur constituency. A nervous Gayatri rushed to her husband, who reacted with perfect equanimity. He calmly told her that this was the only logical outcome of the venture Gayatri had undertaken. Firmly cornered, but lacking in confidence, Gayatri roped Joey in for the State Assembly elections to oppose the home minister of Rajasthan. A reluctant Pat was also dragged in for another parliamentary constituency. Jai asked Devi Singh Mandawa, the president of the Kshatriya Mahasabha, to work actively for Gayatri since she had no experience in politics. Jai, as it were, refused to join active politics himself. However, he accompanied Gayatri on her campaigns.

In one of the few public meetings that Jai addressed, he said:

Loving subjects of Shri Govind Devji,

You all know that this is the realm of Shri Govind Devji Maharaj, and we are his devotees and dewans. When we are protected by Shri Govind Devji and you all love us, we need not be afraid of anything.

The only change that has occurred is that our Chief Minister and other ministers are not as competent as Sir Mirza Ismail and Sir V.T. Krishnamachari were. So it is that your difficulties cannot be so readily removed as before, because these people are not of that calibre. It is difficult to make them understand anything.

The ministers of today feel no responsibility to Rajasthan as a whole. Their vision is limited to their region, city or even their home.

You have seen that with the help of Sukhadiaji (the chief minister who came from Udaipur) Udaipur has become a fine city, while Bikaner and Alwar are neglected. The beautiful and world-famous City of Jaipur is being disfigured by unnecessary demolitions and alterations. Our famous Johri Bazaar has been reduced to the condition of an ordinary Bombay street.

Our Sindhi and Punjabi brothers who have come here (as refugees), after experiencing great difficulties, are still lying on the footpaths...

The Congress has started strange propaganda since the opening of the election campaign. One of the leaders has objected to the candidature of the Maharani of Jaipur... but what about the Maharani of Gwalior? (She was at that time still allied to the Congress.)

We can understand to some extent that they make propaganda against us, but they also make propaganda against the important and honest leaders of their own party out of pure self-interest. You may consider the honesty of this. Many big leaders who worked for the formation of Rajasthan now sit silent or even oppose those in power.

Heera Lal Shastri, the great confidant of Sardar Patel, is silent. The fearless Jai Narain Vyas and Aditendra, one of the organizers of the Congress, are opposing those in the saddle. Why? Because they do not want to become a party to corruption and other evils.

It is no wonder that Rajasthan is suffering. But you are responsible for electing them.

Now the power is in your hands. By now you have the experience to judge who is sincere and honest and who is a cheat.

Jai went on to speak of the good relations between Hindus and Muslims in Jaipur and to remind the people of their religious duties. He also pledged to the government 'on my own behalf and on behalf of all the royalties of Rajasthan that we shall not claim or endeavour to retake what we have relinquished.'

On the eve of the elections, the Congress, the Swatantra Party, and the Jan Sangh organized meetings. Gayatri was apprehensive, since the site chosen for the Swatantra Party meeting could hold as many as 200,000 people. This was much bigger than the places chosen by either the Congress or the Jan Sangh. To her 'amazed pleasure, the ground was completely full'. Jai addressed the crowd and gave a fitting reply to the allegations that he was making his sons contest the election.

Jai said:

> For generations my family had ruled you and we have built up many generations of affection. The new government has taken my State from me, but for all I care, they can take the shirt off my back as long as I can keep that bond of trust and affection. They accuse me of putting up my wife and two of my sons for elections. They say that if I had 176 (the total number of seats being contested for Rajasthan Assembly) sons I would put all of them up too. But they don't know, do they, that I have (gesturing to the entire crowd) more than only 176 sons.

The crowd went delirious. Slogans of 'Maharaja Man Singh *Ki Jai*' rent the air. The crowd rained flowers on Jai and Gayatri. Her victory was assured.

The aura of royalty continued. It was, in fact, growing even as the ugly face of power politics was coming to the fore. Many more people throughout the state were keen to support Gayatri, but were afraid of the government backlash. Jai wanted Gayatri to win by at least 5,000 votes. Jagat sent his good wishes from England, hoping the margin would be at least 1,000.

When the results started pouring in, the winners were stunned. Joey defeated the incumbent home minister. Pat also won his parliamentary seat. In the entire Jaipur district, only one member of the ruling party had been elected. Gayatri defeated her nearest rival by 1,75,000 votes. Every single opponent of Gayatri had to forfeit his deposit.

The victory procession was large, grand, and tumultuous. Jai, along with the family, stood on the balcony of City Palace to watch the procession. He threw gold coins to the people as he used to do in the past. Ma complimented Gayatri for having a husband who supported her in everything. The election result found an entry in the *Guinness Book of World Records*. Gayatri had won by the largest majority ever in a democracy.

Soon thereafter, Jai was elected to the Upper House (Rajya Sabha). When the new members of parliament, gathered to hear the opening address of the president, the central hall included four members of Jai's family—Jai, Gayatri, Pat, and Bubbles (adjutant in the President's Body Guard). Joey was in Jaipur since he had won an assembly seat.

Before Jai and the family could settle into their new jobs, they had to rush back to prepare a welcome for Mrs Jacqueline Kennedy, wife of the President of the United States of America. It was a private visit. Jackie and her sister Lee were planning to visit India. When Jai was informed of the visit, he invited them to Jaipur. A casual invitation was accepted on the spot, and Jaipur was included in the itinerary. The government was still nursing its wounds from the elections and did not want any publicity to go to the Jaipur House. The sentiment was conveyed to the then ambassador of the United States in India, John Kenneth Galbraith, who communicated the same to President Kennedy. The president replied that he never interfered with his wife's private arrangements. Thus, despite opposition from all around, Jackie's visit was on. Even on her arrival at Jaipur, there were reservations regarding her visit to City Palace. In fact, Jackie had been told that she was not allowed to go there. Jackie was interested in arts, and it would have been impolite not to take her to the City Palace Museum. The situation was piquant: a reluctant administration resisting a guest's desire. Finally, she was taken to City Palace, but at night.

Later, Galbraith commented in one of his books (*An Ambassador's Journal*) that Jai and his family tried to get political mileage out of this visit. In retrospect it sounds preposterous—to look for political gains from the visit of the wife of a president of a distant country, when more than half the family had broken a record of sorts by winning elections by a landslide majority. While departing, Jackie extended an invitation to Jai and Gayatri to come and stay with them in Washington.

Jai had, meanwhile, established a charitable trust in the name of Maharaja Sawai Jai Singh and was paying an annual amount of Rs 1,50,000 from his privy purse to it. Gayatri, as an elected representative, made good use of this trust to ameliorate the conditions of the poor.

Thereafter, Jai went off to England. For the first time, Gayatri had to stay back to attend to her parliamentary duties, as also to campaign for candidates in the parliamentary by-elections. Immediately after the by-polls, she joined Jai in England. She got the news of the victory of the Swatantra Party candidate for whom she had campaigned, while having dinner with the Dutch Ambassador in London. She was elated and recalls that triumphant moment till date.

In October, Jai and Gayatri left for America. After visiting New York and Virginia, they reached Washington. They were put up at Blair House as the president's guests. The Cuban crisis broke out just then, and the dance party arranged by the president in their honour had to be cancelled. Instead a small dinner party was hosted. President Kennedy chided Gayatri, 'I hear you are the Barry Goldwater of India.' He introduced her to the senators as 'the woman with the most staggering majority that anyone has ever earned in an election.'

Jai and Gayatri were in New York when the war broke out between China and India. Gayatri wanted to return home immediately, but Jai prevailed saying that a change in their programme could not possibly make a difference to the situation in India. On their return, both participated in the post-war proceedings of the Houses: Gayatri in the Lok Sabha and Jai in the Rajya Sabha. As was his wont, Jai made concrete suggestions and propounded his philosophy of compromise. Gayatri, on the other hand, went for Nehru's jugular blaming him for the 'mess'. Nehru responded by saying, 'I will not bandy words with a lady.'

The next year, Jai again went to England alone, from where he wrote to Gayatri:

My Darling Love,

Darling, what a party we had last night. Something one hears about but seldom sees. Most glamorous and colourful. The Queen looked wonderful and so did Princess Alexandra. There were about 20 other Royals... Darling, it is wonderful to be here, but I am very worried about you and your stupid tours all over the place in this heat. Please Darling look after yourself—for someone who lives for you alone—and come soon. You need a holiday badly. See you on the ninth—our day!!

Yours only,
Jai

Prince Philip visited Jaipur in March 1965 and stayed with Jai and Gayatri for one week. Fortunately, no motives were attributed to nor protests registered against this visit. Philip later said of Jai:

I have met many people who could be described as charming, but few, if any, had quite Jai's special brand of kindly charm and gentleness of character. Together with his exceptionally beautiful and talented wife, Ayesha, they made the most delightful hosts. Always thoughtful and considerate, they had a genius for generating a light-hearted gaiety wherever they chose to entertain their friends. Kipling may have written, 'East is East, and West is West, and never the twain shall meet,' but anyone who ever had the pleasure of staying with Jai and Ayesha in India knows that they had a magic ability of making 'the twain meet' in the most delightful way.

While at Jaipur, Prince Philip participated in the celebrations of the festival of Holi in City Palace. He was so thrilled to have been a part of the festivities that he wrote to Gayatri from the President's House at Rawalpindi:

> ...I have never experienced anything like last week in my whole life. Every moment was sheer joy and it's only the bruises from polo and the pink stain on my fingers which remain to convince me that the whole thing wasn't some marvellous dream.

He had later commented that to experience the festival of Holi in Jaipur in the company of Jai and Gayatri was to gain a glimpse of the universality of mankind.

A year later, Prince Philip, while flying in an airplane, cabled:

> From the Duke of Edinburgh, a multi-coloured Holi to you all...Christopher, Joe, Sarah and I are green with envy and pink with nostalgia.
>
> Philip.

---

1 He even died early, in 1997, at the age of 48.

2 The full version is: when on the eve of the constitution being finally adopted the rulers, with the exception of two or three, accepted the same as binding upon

them and their states, it must follow that they accepted and adopted the Constitution of India because they thought and were assured that the provisions in it regarding themselves and their successors were to their satisfaction and were binding in nature. They certainly never imagined ...

3   It was known as Maji Ka Bag. Later, the British Resident stayed here, hence, the name, changed to the Residency. During Mickey's marriage, the princes stayed here, hence, it was re-christened as Princes' Hostel. When Jai moved to this place in 1958, it was called Rajmahal. It is now being run as a hotel.

4   The Fauna Preservation Society of London referred the question of the propriety of this shoot to E.P. Gee, a great authority on wildlife in India. He replied that the 'tiger is not a protected species in India and the shooting of a tiger by the Royal Party would be just the same as shooting a stag in Scotland and therefore it should not be frowned upon'.

AMBASSADOR TO SPAIN

Prime Minister Shastri once again offered an ambassadorship to Jai. He gave him a choice of three countries. Jai had earlier refused the same assignment to Argentina. However, this time he said yes and chose Spain. Kachhwahas, from Man Singh to Sawai Man Singh had all been excellent diplomats besides being brave warriors. Jai, with his upbringing, was absolutely suited for the job. He could, it was said, charm a vulture off a corpse.

Before leaving for Spain in October 1965, he called the Rajputs of Jaipur and gave them a piece of his mind. He admonished them for neither taking the political lead that Gayatri and his sons had given, nor being steadfast in their support. He also admonished them for their 'obstinate and childlike attitude against giving up old, outdated and outmoded ideas and ways of life'. He touched on the constant rivalry between the Rajputs and the Jats. He said:

> It is indeed heartbreaking and tragic to have to admit that perhaps no other community with such a glorious past has shown more lack of organization, cooperation, unity and courage than the Rajputs. A number of jagirdars had voluntarily taken me to their *thikanas*, stood

on the same platform and in public pledged us and our cause full support. Then after a few days, they have come to say how terribly sorry they were as they now find they cannot associate themselves with us or our party, as the chief minister called them and told them that unless they dissociate themselves from all activities of the maharaja and the maharani, their compensations will be affected. So those very people, who with great enthusiasm took us to their homes, now asked to be pardoned and excused, but at the same time had the audacity to assure me of their continued loyalty and service like their forefathers.

What was stranger still, to continue the rout, others forgetting all age-old and honoured social ties and demands of normal hospitality conveniently left their houses so as to be conveniently absent when Her Highness addressed public meetings in their towns and villages. Where would a General have stood, what would have been his plight if his allies, his commanders, his troops and followers had thus deserted him on the eve of battle?

Nothing has shocked me more or shaken my faith in the Rajput community than this defeatist if not cowardly attitude...and I see little future in myself or, for that matter, in anyone else shouldering the dubious and uncertain responsibilities of Rajput leadership at a time when, alas, Rajput chivalry, unity and courage appear at their lowest ebb.

After weeks and months of careful thought I am convinced that I can serve our country better in other ways than by remaining and vegetating in the senseless and useless morass of the petty local politics of Rajasthan.

Rajputs can, I am confident, play a great part in the shaping of the future of our state and the country as a whole. Unfortunately, it appears to be the avowed policy of the authorities that they are neither given a fair opportunity nor trusted. This obvious partiality, injustice and step-motherly treatment greatly affects their morale and sense of responsibility.

Justice cannot be obtained by any but the favoured few. Their forbearance might, now that I am away, snap under the strain of such planned and persistent persecution and perhaps, eventually, even take the form of a demand for a separate Rajput state as is now being voiced regarding the creation of a Punjabi Suba. The disastrous consequences of such a move can well be imagined.

The nobles of Jaipur were opposed to Jai taking up the new assignment primarily because the threat to the privy purses was looming large. Jai had a high stature and was a pillar of strength. The other princes felt almost orphaned in his absence. Nonetheless, Jai left for Spain as scheduled, despite all opposition. Gayatri again stayed back to attend to her parliamentary duties. On 29 October 1965, he wrote to Gayatri:

My darling Angel,

It was wonderful leaving Delhi and I have never been in happier mood but you, little Pat, upset the apple cart in Bombay! I never like seeing you upset, the most beautiful woman in the world. You may not realize it but, Darling, all my success in life has been because of your unswerving support with love and devotion.

I can never forget the sight of you standing on the pier at Bombay, waving at me as I sailed for the Middle East in 1941. You alone supported me as a brave Rajput wife should, when the rest of the family condemned me and my love. I can never reward you enough for your courage and devotion. No words of mine can adequately express my feelings, but I know you will understand what I mean. Just remember I will always stand by you and never never let you down, whatever sacrifice it may entail for my lifelong companion.

Look after yourself little girl and come to Madrid soon, where I will be waiting to greet you with loving arms.

All my love Darling from your devoted
Jai

Jai joined his duties formally at Madrid. But he was alone and was missing Gayatri. He wrote:

My darling love,

Here I am at last with flashes of bulbs and cameras and gay parties.
I had a wonderful reception. Am keeping all the papers with my
photos for you or shall I send them so you can practise your
Spanish!! Darling, it's wonderful here but please come soon as I
need your help and charm in my duties.

Hope you are not working too hard and making too many
speeches. Please see the PM helps your career.

All my love Darling and miss you more than I can say.

Yours only
Jai

Jai was the first ambassador sent by India to Spain, so for the
first few months he had to stay in a hotel. Once Gayatri (and
subsequently Jagat) joined him, they moved into a flat. With
Jai and Gayatri around, the social circuit could not but warm
up. The Spaniards and Jai shared a love for polo and shooting.
Jai did not play polo as frequently, but he used to umpire
regularly. Jai was known for his extreme fairness as an umpire.
Being a gentleman, Jai was a natural diplomat. However, the
Spaniards found one of his habits rather strange. Jai used to
go out jogging everyday. This was a novel sight for the
Spaniards. One of them commented: 'Who can that strange
gypsy be? I see him running through the streets every morning.'

There were no Indians in Spain except in the Balearic and
Canary Islands, to which Jai paid regular visits. Quentin
Crewe in *The Last Maharaja* records a touching episode:

There was one old Indian tailor living in the south of Spain, who
appeared one day in Madrid and asked to see the ambassador. He
told Jai that he had lived in Spain for 50 years and that soon he
would die. Before dying, he wanted one last, real Indian meal to
remind him of his youth. Where could he get it? 'You shall have it
here,' said Jai. The next day, Jai told his guests that lunch would be

an hour later than usual. The tailor was given a huge feast in the
ambassador's dining room. When he came out, he touched Jai's feet
and went away and was never heard of again.

There is no doubt that Jai did a good job for India in Spain.
India meant nothing to most Spaniards when he took over but
this perception changed. Lord Roderick Pratt, who went to
stay with Jai in Madrid, remembers that everybody seemed
to know him, including the police, who chased his speeding
car as he was showing Lord and Lady Roderick around
Madrid on their first evening. When they caught him, the
police laughed and saluted him. It was like the days when
Jai was chased into Knightsbridge Barracks. He had not
changed a bit.

Gayatri was now a member of parliament, and she had to
frequently come back to India to attend to her duties. Jai
wrote to her as often as possible. In January 1967, he wrote:

> How is the busy Queen doing? Hope not overworked with the
> problems of Rajasthan. Life is gay as we are having many farewell
> parties for the Pakistani Ambassador. Have had some good shoots.
> Vulchis asked me to go this weekend, but duty does not permit!
> Don't laugh!

Later, he wrote in April:

> I had a very gay time in Barcelona and won two prizes. I hope you
> will arrange for good Indian dancers to come, as I am sure they will
> be very popular. All my love darling and come soon. The house is so
> empty without you, my love, and my success at entertaining not so
> good!! So happy the boys have been good. Please look after them
> and keep them on the right path.

During Jai's stay in Spain, he opened the Hispano-Indian
Chamber. It was during this time that Lal Bahadur Shastri
died. On the whole, Jai was happy to be away from the
unpalatable political scene in India. Although he missed

Gayatri, he was having a good time. Troubled about some violent protests in Delhi, he expressed his anguish to her: 'You can imagine how worrying it is when one is so far away. Come soon in this happy atmosphere as I long to have you with me.'

Jai had, in the meanwhile, moved into a beautiful house in Amador de los Rios. Whenever Gayatri would be in Spain, they would constantly tour the countryside. They were also an inseparable part of the soirées. Whenever Gayatri was not there, Jai's letters to her were happy in tone, but always imbued with expression of feelings that he missed her.

Jai and Gayatri celebrated their silver wedding anniversary on 9 May 1965. Although, they were apart for most of the year, they met on 9 May at Cannes where Jai had moved to revive polo. Jai joked: 'Don't tell me I have actually managed to put up with you for 25 years.' Ma was always appreciative of Jai, reminding Gayatri how lucky she was to have a husband who gave her so much freedom and encouraged her in all her projects. Contraindications were few and far between and were always for a good reason.

In 1965, Bhawani Singh (Bubbles) married Princess Padmani Kumari, daughter of His Highness Shri Rajendra Prakash of Sirmaur. Gayatri's sister, Ila, and her brother, Inderjeet, had already died. In the middle of the celebrations of Bubbles' marriage, Bhaiya, her elder brother suffered a serious accident in a polo match. He never regained his health and remained a vegetable for the rest of his life. Gayatri was shattered but weathered over the trauma with Jai, who proved to be a pillar of strength, providing strong support and comfort.

There was another round of elections in 1967. The boundaries of Jaipur had been deliberately gerrymandered. The aim was not to let Gayatri have the advantage of the

Jaipur electorate. Electioneering became much more hectic and tiring, with only a small part of Jaipur City falling in Gayatri's constituency. Pat and Joey were disillusioned with politics and refused to contest the next elections. During this campaign, Jai stayed in Madrid. Gayatri spoke to him everyday. When she was down with fever, Jai asked Pat to send his wife (who was Ila's daughter) and his son, to Gayatri, to keep her company.

When the results were declared, Gayatri had retained her parliamentary seat. The opposition parties in the state government had won more than the ruling party. However, Governor Sri Sampuranand delayed inviting the opposition; and the ruling party began its manipulations. Gayatri kept the elected members in City Palace for one night and shifted them to Kanota Fort (about 20 kms from Jaipur) the next day. The governor resorted to a stratagem. He imposed prohibitory orders (not allowing more than five persons to get together at one place) in Civil Lines, where he and the ministers stayed, and then invited the minority to form the government. There were massive protests. For the first time in the history of Jaipur, a curfew had to be imposed in the entire city. Jai returned to India. He flew to Delhi with Gayatri to meet President Dr. S. Radhakrishnan and Home Minister Yashwant Rao Chauhan. On their assurance that peace would prevail, curfew was lifted. The orders regarding the lifting of the curfew had not trickled down to some policeman. In the ensuing confusion, the police shot dead nine people. Forty-nine people were wounded. Democracy was becoming dangerously frightening.

The assembly was to meet six days later and the opposition coalition was intact. However, president's rule was imposed in the State of Rajasthan for a month and half. This was to give

time to the minority party to lure away the members of
Gayatri's coalition.

With the assembly in animated suspension, Gayatri had
little to do. She joined Jai in Spain. Blandishments were
offered to Gayatri's coalition members and defections
followed. Indian politics was in an abyss. Gayatri was
disillusioned and so was Jai.

A year before these elections, a resolution had been moved
for the first time for the abolition of privy purses in the
Congress Party Convention in 1966. The politician's barbs in
the election campaigns were towards the princes, exhorting
the public to ask the maharajas: 'How many wells were dug
and roads made during their rule?'

But it is a point of fact that metalled roads had doubled in
Jai's time and so had railway tracks. Nonetheless, the
Congress adopted the abolition of privy purses as a resolution
and also decided to stop all privileges of the princes as
'incongruous to the concept and practice of democracy'.

Meanwhile, Ma took seriously ill. Gayatri decided to fly to
Bombay to see her. Gayatri was waiting in Delhi at the airport
when she received the information that Ma had died.

Gayatri joined Jai in Spain again after Ma's death.
Unwarranted sniping at Jai's tenure in Spain, as also the
precarious position of the princes back home, persuaded Jai to
seek his return to India. In fact, the mud slinging against the
princes was at its worst. As Gaj Singh of Jodhpur said, 'From
being privileged, we became untouchables. A lot of
propaganda was whipped up against us, which made the
simplest activity suspect.' It was almost as if a public
campaign had been launched to paint the princes as
decadent, exploitative, and anti-democratic. On the subject of
democracy, the politically untutored Maharaja of Jodhpur had

humiliated the mighty political organization of the Congress by sweeping the board in the first election itself. A majority of the maharajas who stood for elections also won their seats. Bibhukumari Devi, the Maharani of Tripura, explains: 'For a section of people, we are very dear. Basically they know, we won't cheat them and won't make money at their expense.' Jagat Mehta, the former Indian foreign secretary, whose father had worked for the Maharaja of Udaipur, endorses that position: 'Maharajas appear so much more benign, so much more restrained than today's corrupt politicians.'

However, in keeping with the times, Jai too was made a target of baseless allegations. He was blamed, among other things, for being away from Madrid for prolonged periods. This allegation was made in the face of express government instructions to Jai that he should try and exploit his personal contacts in Europe for the purchase of arms for India. Even then, Jai's absence from Madrid was only for seven weeks in one year. A public servant gets more leave.

Jai thought enough was enough. He decided to return to Delhi.

THE LAST PHASE

A Concord of Princes, ostensibly to defend their interests but more particularly, to fight against the abolition of the privy purses, was founded. However, the princes as usual could not agree on any single line of action. Even if they did, there was little they could do. As Crewe says:

> There was a certain amount of talk about secession, but everyone knew that this was unrealistic. The princes' case, while morally correct, was hopeless. They had nothing to bargain with, as they had given away everything in exchange for promises. The government's case was indefensible by honourable standards, but had a cold logic behind it. Backed by vindictiveness and reinforced by power, the government could not fail to win in the end.

Jai always participated in the proceedings of the Concord, going with the majority. He chose the path of least resistance deliberately and out of practical considerations. At stake were privileges, like flying flags on cars, a public holiday on the king's birthday, military honours at funerals and gun salutes, besides the purse itself. In one of the discussions, the Maharana of Udaipur wondered 'whether it would be worthwhile for me to live, whether I would deserve to live, whether those who value history and tradition would own me as an Indian if I were to acquiesce in the derogation of this Institution? It is not my private possession. I am a trustee and a servant. Hardships are to be endured but not dishonour.' On the other hand was Dr Karni Singh, the Maharaja of Bikaner, who had been a member of parliament since 1952. He was, personally, not opposed to the abolition of privy purses, since he felt that after their abolition 'the former rulers would cease to be the government's whipping boys.'

But all the effort seemed to be falling through a sieve. The disenchantment was fuelled by the regime in Rajasthan, which Gayatri had vowed to overthrow at any cost. A lengthy column in a Bombay newspaper ran a report on Jai's disillusionment and his intentions to join active politics. As the paper said, 'If he did, it would be a shattering blow for the Congress.' An effort was ostensibly being made to cobble together a conglomerate of the princes. Prominent Jat leaders were also approached. But ultimately nothing came out of it. It is not clear whether Jai was keen to join active politics or not. While Devi Singh Mandawa said that such a plan was on, Gayatri recollects that Jai was toying with the idea of handing over everything to his sons and retiring to England.

Besides the larger problems, Jai had to face the obscurantist attitude of the regime in Rajasthan on trivial issues. Jai had a marble statue made of Sawai Jai Singh, the founder of Jaipur City. He wanted the president of India to personalty inaugurate the installation of the statue. The formal channel through the state government was deliberately clogged. Finally, Jai had to approach President Zakir Hussain directly. The president graciously consented and unveiled the statue.

At this time, Jai also decided to have a smaller house,

constructed on the grounds of Ram Bagh. He called it Lily Pool where Gayatri lives till date.

As usual, Jai and Gayatri left for England in May 1969. Jai judged a horse show at Windsor. He and Gayatri travelled a lot, visiting Spain, Argentina, Venezuela, and Brazil, while simultaneously following the polo circuit. This time, events were really crammed in. Gayatri recollects: 'I don't really believe in premonitions, but that summer I was plagued by a haunting feeling that somehow our time was running out and we should do as much, and see as much, as we could reasonably manage.'

Upon their return, Gayatri stayed in Delhi, and Jai returned to Jaipur. On one occasion, Jai fainted. The cardiologist suggested rest. Even though Jai confessed that he felt tired at times, he scoffed at the doctor's advice as 'all the silly fuss about nothing'. But the deterioration in his health was .too conspicuous. Pandit Heera Lal Shastri, the former chief minister wrote to Jai on 5 April 1970:

> The other day, I happened to be walking outside the Jaipur Airport when somebody told me that you were due to fly to Bombay the same morning. When I came in, I just had a glimpse from a distance: you were already walking towards the airport. People who saw you from near told me that you looked very weak. From your gait I too thought that you were not your usual self. I would, therefore, come to you some day. Also the 'Churma-dal-bati'[1] business has all along been waiting for you. I wonder if you realize I am so deeply attached to your person.

Jai never heeded any advice to rest. He went to Kota in January 1970 to condole the death of his aunt, the Rajmata of Kota. His cousin and PS, Dalel Singh, was solicitous about his health. Jai laughed: 'Do you want me to die in bed? I want to die on the battlefield, and the polo field is my battlefield.'

Ignoring doctors' advice, he went on to play polo with the 61st Cavalry at Calcutta. They won the Indian Polo Association Cup, the highest award in India. Jai and Gayatri stayed in Calcutta with Bhaiya (Gayatri's brother). Gayatri had to undergo a major operation in Bombay in April 1970. While she was convalescing in Bombay, Bhaiya died. Bhaiya was not only close to Gayatri but was one of Jai's closest friends. Bhaiya's death forced Jai to cancel his meeting with the home minister over the subject of privy purses. But he wrote a letter saying:

> I have read the letters addressed by the Rulers of Baroda and Dharangadhra to the President of India, and I wholly associate myself with them. It is now for the consideration of the president and the government to refer the question to the Supreme Court for its advisory opinion. I do not know what the strict interpretation of the law might be. But I must put it to you, with all the force at my command, that it is the intention of the Constitution and the spirit of the law that must count... If the rulers, or for that matter anyone else, are denied even a judicial hearing it will not redound to our national credit or to the prestige of the government.

Since the government was on the verge of introducing the bill for abolition of privy purses in parliament, Jai had to make strenuous efforts to persuade the government in Delhi to recognize Bhaiya's nephew (Inderjeet's son) as the Maharaja of Cooch Behar.

The blooming of jacarandas in May heralded the time for Jai to pack up and leave for England. This time Gayatri wanted him to stay on till their wedding anniversary. She herself could not go because of her parliamentary duties. However, instead of celebrating their anniversary by the Christian calendar, they celebrated the same by the lunar calendar. Jai left for England on 7 May 1970. Gayatri followed him on the 23rd May in time for her 51st birthday. At this time, Jai was 59.

Before his departure for England, Jai had a drink with Yashwant Rao Pawar of Dewas Jr, at Jai's house in Delhi on 33, Aurangzeb Road. On being advised to cut down on his physical activities on the polo field on account of his health, Jai responded with prophetic words:

> Bhausaheb Dada, I know what you say is out of your affection for me and I assure you I have always valued the same. Perhaps you are right; but then polo was my first and true love and the only one in which I have achieved a part of my ambitions. Knowing as you do what the game means to me in every sense of the word, I ask you: what more can I now ask for or expect of life? Therefore, my last wish is that my end should come on the polo field, in the midst of a chukka, with my friends around me, my pony under me, my polo stick in my hand and my boots on.

The government had introduced the bill on privy purses on 18 May, but Gayatri left despite opposition from all around. When she reached England, the usual round of parties started. Jai was now playing less and umpiring more. His handicap was down to three.

While umpiring at Windsor, Jai had a nasty fall. Gayatri for a while toyed with the idea of cancelling the cocktails at King's Beeches, which Jai and Gayatri had been hosting every year after the finals of the Queen's Cup. Jai insisted that the show must go on. The Queen and Prince Philip used to come to this party every year. This time, Lord Mountbatten was also present. Jai and Dicky had a long chat on the situation in India. When Jai told Dicky about the government's attempt to humiliate the former rulers, Dicky commented that Jai was not the kind of person who could be humiliated. They decided to talk more, later.

The British parliamentary elections were due when Ascot week began. Jai umpired throughout the tournament and did not play himself. However, he announced his intention to resume the game at Cirencester.

The first match at Cirencester was on 24 June 1970. It was a depressing day—grey, windy, and drizzling. Jai was playing after quite a hiatus. The game was also slow and unexciting. Bubbles and Gayatri were both watching Jai from the car when suddenly, Jai fell from his pony without warning.

He was rushed to the hospital, where he was pronounced dead on arrival.

---

1 *Churma-dal-bati* is a Rajasthani speciality. *Churma* is crushed flour roti that is sweetened, *dal* (cereals)and *bati* is made of flour, and is round like a ball, unlike a roti which is round and flat. The preparation is made on festive occasions and for guests.

POSTSCRIPT

The news of Jai's death moved Jaipur as nothing else could have. His body was to be flown into the city on 25 June. The public started gathering at Sanganer Airport in the morning. They continued to wait through the day, braving the scorching sun of June in Jaipur. It seemed like a hideous nightmare. Their beloved Maharaja was coming home, but in a coffin. They were all in a trance, refusing to believe the reality.

The Indian Airlines plane, *Rameshwaram*, appeared in the sky at 6.35 p.m. The surging mass of humanity gathered at the airport went silent. It all seemed so surreal. Time seemed to stop, and the air was still. There was pindrop silence at the airport when the plane came to a halt at 6.40 p.m.

The first to step out was a grief-stricken Gayatri Devi, barely 51, and already a rajmata. Maharaj Kumar Bhawani Singh followed with his younger brother Maharaj Kumar Jagat Singh carrying the ever-smiling Jai in a sandalwood coffin, frozen in the still serenity of death. The 61st Cavalary (earlier the Jaipur Cavalary) presented a Guard of Honour. The coffin was hoisted atop a gun carriage to be carried to City Palace,

14 kms away. The entire route from Sanganer Airport to City Palace swarmed with people wanting to pay their last respects, and who stopped the carriage every 10 yards.

On arrival of the cortege at City Palace, Jai's body was placed on a raised platform in Chandra Mahal, opposite the Govind Dev Temple. Mourners, driven by an irresistible desire for a last *darshan*, filed past throughout the night. The body lay in state for the whole of the next day. Jai's four sons Bhawani, Joey, Pat, and Jagat kept constant vigil.

On 27 June 1970, the funeral procession began at 9 a.m. A 19-gun salute was fired from Nahargarh. Jai's body was taken on a gun carriage. Three caparisoned elephants led the procession. The mahout on the first elephant carried the *Mah-e-Murtib*, a golden rod[1], which had been given by the Mughals to the rulers of Amber as a token of special distinction and honour. The mahouts of the other two elephants were throwing coins to the crowds. Elephants were followed by camels, another row of elephants, horse chariots, the police band (their instruments draped in black), and soldiers from various regiments. The palace officials were in white, even their swords were sheathed in white. After them came 20 royal priests with shaven heads, followed by a truck carrying flowers and wreaths. The gun carriage carrying Jai's body was at the end, followed by Jai's sons, the nobles of Rajputana, and political bigwigs.

The most heartrending sight in the entire procession was that of Zorawar, Jai's polo horse. The riderless horse carried the cap and the 15 medals of his master.

The one-mile-long procession took two hours to reach Gatore, the cremation ground of the royal family. En route, each terrace, balcony and window was bulging with mourning throngs. They also clung to trees and telegraph poles. There were 500,000 people occupying vantage points in the area surrounding the cremation ground. Many had come from remote villages, 20 to 30 miles away, on foot or on bullock carts to pay their homage. There was not an inch of space available anywhere. It was the largest gathering ever in Jaipur.

The pyre was lit by the then Maharaj Kumar Bhawani Singh, the heir apparent. The funeral, unprecedented in many ways, was the first ever where the heir apparent performed the last rites.[2] The hills echoed with a 19-gun salute. The crowd rent the air with slogans of 'Maharaja ki Jai' and 'Maharaja amar rahe'.

Gayatri said: 'From my room in City Palace, I heard the sound of the guns, as Bubbles set light to the funeral pyre. I could hear, too, the sounds of the wailing, and grief seized me almost like a physical spasm.'

The funeral was the proof, if proof was required, of the strong bond that existed between Jai and his people, which had grown stronger after Independence. There was no doubt that if Jai had entered politics, as was being speculated, he would have decimated firmly entrenched citadels. However, in the circumstances, the inverterate politicians almost heaved a sigh of relief.

The press also poured its grief. 'He played the game and played it fair,' said *The Statesman*. Mourning the passing away of the 'debonair' maharaja, *The Statesman* went on, 'there is no doubt that he had a large measure of sympathy for the underdog and a fund of goodwill towards everybody.'

The Hindustan Times spoke of the urbane and generous maharaja who was immensely lovable and a benign head. *The Times of India*, applauding his 'democratic outlook', said, 'Maharaja Man Singh, a constitutional reformer, synthesized monarchy with democracy and functioned through his

Council of State as a constitutionalist and a trustee of the people.' *The Rajasthan Chronicle* under the headline 'Pink City Shocked' called him the architect of modern Jaipur.

The world press paid generous tributes. *The Daily Telegraph,* in an article titled the 'Modest Prince', pointed out: 'In two months the Maharani of Jaipur has lost both her brother, the Maharaja of Cooch Behar, and now her husband through injuries at polo. It is 100 years on Sunday since the game arrived from India.' *The Times* was effusive about Jai's Commission in the Guards in 1939, as also his participation in World War II. His contribution to polo, was of course, remembered in every single tribute.

La Vanguardia Espanola (Spain), in an article titled, 'The passing away of a great prince—Man Singh, Maharaja of Jaipur' said:

> He was an international figure being the ruler of one of the most ancient dynasties. He played an important role together with Lord Mountbatten during the crucial times of Indian Independence, being one of the first rulers who signed the Instrument of Accession. Later, he was made the Rajpramukh of Rajasthan, thus making Jaipur the premier State of Rajasthan. A writer commenting on his transition from absolute monarchy to complete democracy said he had done it as easily and quickly as he changed ponies at a polo match.
>
> The ones who knew him always remember his kindness, generosity, his warm smile, and the modesty with which he received the applause of his admirers. Wherever it was, whether in London, Madrid, the Riviera or Delhi, he was the cynosure of all eyes and could never be unnoticed.

A month later, a memorial service was held in the Guards' Chapel at London. Gayatri, Jagat and Maharaja Gaj Singh of Jodhpur attended it. Dicky Mountbatten read the tribute to Jai, though he was ill and had been advised rest by his doctors:

This Act of Tribute to the late Maharaja of Jaipur is being held in the Guards' Chapel as it has been organized by the Life Guards in memory of one of the most remarkable and unusual officers ever to hold a Commission in the Regiment. This fact is in itself unique since none of the hundreds of other Ruling Princes of India have had this tribute paid to them. We had been close friends for the last 37 years.

Dicky then went on to speak about Jai's life and contribution to Jaipur. Recalling his visit to Jaipur on the Silver Jubilee celebrations of Jai's coronation, he said:

On that state visit, I also took the salute when the Sawai Man Guards Regiment trooped the Colour. None of our foot-guard regiments could have done it any better. Indeed it was the Jaipur Guards' reputation for smartness that led me to select them as one of the units to re-occupy Hong Kong when it was liberated from the Japanese. When I visited them there I was gratified to find what a deep and favourable impression they were making. That was Jai all over.

Recalling the period of parleys in 1947, Dicky said:

When the transfer of power and partition of India came, Jai and his State were a model of intelligent, loyal cooperation and understanding, much as they must have disliked it. During the recurring communal riots and massacres, which had started many months before I became viceroy and rose to their greatest pitch after the transfer of power, Jaipur remained splendidly free of communal troubles. Jai himself patrolled the streets at night to ensure that no trouble flared up, as was occurring in other nearby areas.

In a letter to the editor of one of the leading Indian newspapers, a member of the Rajya Sabha pointed out that Jai had shown the way to deal with communalism by treating all his subjects with equal fairness regardless of caste or religion. I strongly endorse this.

John Gunther wrote of Jai's wonderful acceptance of the new order which entailed the bitter loss of ruling powers: 'The Maharaja changed over to a new setting with the same ease with which he changed his ponies in a Polo match.'

Dicky summed up by describing the funeral accorded to Jai:

> The government gave their full cooperation for a proper State
> Funeral at which his erstwhile subjects showed their respect,
> affection and indeed their love for their maharaja. The papers
> report that the crowds chanted 'Maharaja Man Singh ki Jai', the
> traditional cry of affection and veneration. Jai's body has been
> cremated, but his indomitable spirit lives on in their hearts and in
> ours. So may I end by re-echoing the cry: 'Maharaja Man Singh
> ki Jai'.

Dicky later came to the flat with Gayatri and comforted her.
As she recollects, 'His words of comfort got through to me and
gave me my first, though still tremulous, confidence about
facing the future and living out the rest of my life without Jai.'

P.G. Pulambo, an old friend, said:

> It would be relatively easy, by stringing together a few hyperboles, to
> paint well enough a prosaic portrait of the man we all knew simply
> as Jai. To delve deeper, to endeavour to describe his unique
> personality is altogether different, involving of necessity a
> summation of those evanescent impressions which seem etched in
> the unconscious until we reach out to grasp them, when they
> fragment like quicksilver to the touch.
>
> The love and respect in which he was held by his people and
> by his friends and his zest for life are legendary. But, perhaps
> his greatness as a man stemmed from an essential humanity, of
> which nobody who met him could fail to be aware, and from his
> serene outlook, induced by some inner contentment, which
> permitted him like the lotus flower, to sit in the water and never get
> wet. A total lack of arrogance in one boasting a fraction of his power
> and achievements would have been remarkable. In Jai, it was
> ineffable.
>
> In these times we speak very occasionally of a man who seems
> to us to transcend his age with a timeless quality which gives him a
> dimension unattainable by ordinary men. To this very select

company Jai belonged, not merely a man for all seasons, not merely a man of his time, but a man for all time.

The Duke of Edinburgh, Prince Philip wrote:

I am not going to try to guess what Jai meant to other people or what sort of contribution he made to life. All I know is that I gained immeasurably from his friendship in all sorts of circumstances; in the things we did together, like playing polo or shooting or just sitting and chatting under the moon in Jaipur or in a country house in England.

To me Jai had a serene quality, a sort of cheerful calm which may well have been exasperating for some, but to me it was a most endearing and enjoyable characteristic. He combined with that a very rare quality in men, he was supremely civilized. Kind and modest, but with an unerring instinct for the highest standards of human ambition and behaviour.

Perhaps this is a prejudiced view but then friendship is prejudice.

Three months after Jai's death, a bill was introduced in the Lok Sabha for the abolition of privy purses. It was passed by the requisite two-thirds majority in the Lok Sabha, but was rejected in the Rajya Sabha.

The government then used the intelligent stratagem of bringing to life an innocuous clause in the covenant signed between the rulers and the government in 1947. It enabled the president to de-recognize a prince who grossly misbehaved or committed a serious crime. The president wrote to each of the princes, de-recognizing each of them on 6 September 1970.

The princes went to the Supreme Court and promptly got themselves restored. An 11-judge bench of the Supreme Court of India rapped the government on the knuckles. Justice K.S. Hegde remarked:

The question whether the rulers can be de-recognized by the president is of secondary importance. What is of utmost importance for the future of our democracy is whether the Executive in this country can flout the mandates of the Constitution and set at naught Legislative enactments at its discretion. If it is held that it can, then our hitherto held assumption, that in this country we are ruled by laws and not by men and women, must be given up as erroneous.

An editorial commented that no rational citizen of this country could disagree with the observations of Shri C. Rajagopalachari, the doyen of India's statesmen, on the judgment: 'The Supreme Court has, if I may so say respectfully justified its existence. It has saved India's honour. The Court has justified the people's confidence in it as an impregnable bulwark for safeguarding justice and democracy against authoritarianism.' Justice Shri K. Santhanam opined that the whole episode of de-recognizing the princes was rather hopelessly reckless and irresponsible.

It was rather unfortunate that in their zeal for more powers and a flair for 'instant socialism', those in authority wanted to de-recognize the whole princely order, their privy purse, and privileges. However laudable the objectives may be, persons in authority have to respect the Constitutional rights of any citizen of India, be he a prince or a pauper. The Supreme Court had once again vindicated the Constitution by its historic judgment in the princes' case, with nine out of 11 judges striking down the impugned presidential order de-recognizing the princes.

But the remission was short. Elections were held in February 1971, one year ahead of schedule. Predictably, the ruling party returned to power with the requisite majority. Both Houses of Parliament passed the 26th amendment which received the assent of the president on 28 December 1971.

Effective this date, royalty ceased to exist in India.

However, Jai lived on in the minds of the people. Few people have achieved the distinction of becoming legends in their lifetime. Jai, a prince, a ruler, a soldier, a sportsman, a diplomat and above all, a sterling human being, became a legend. Rajmal Surana, the doyen of the jeweller's fraternity in Jaipur, recollects:

> It was in 1932 when he was invested with full powers that I had the privilege of meeting him with a deputation. It was the period when every state had its own customs. The minority administration imposed import duty on jewellery. This had hampered the business greatly. The entire position was explained to him and he was reminded that it was Maharaja Sawai Jai Singhji who had invited the jewellers and cutters to settle down at Jaipur when it was founded. After patiently hearing us, he realized our hardships. He made a very pertinent remark that if the jewellery trade disappeared from Jaipur there would be very little left there.
>
> Had he not taken that decision at that time, the depression of the latter period would have ruined the trade entirely and today there would not have been a single jeweller left in Jaipur City. It is due to his sagacious action that this state, which today employs more than 30,000 families in the jewellery trade, was saved. And today we can boast that Jaipur stands first as far as cutting and polishing of rare and precious stones is concerned. It is one of the biggest industries in the entire country. This one incident should be quite sufficient to illustrate his wisdom and farsightedness.

Gayatri does not tire of quoting what Jai used to tell her often, 'We are what we are, because of Jaipur and we must give back what we got.' Posters, stray cattle, encroachments, and filth were foreign to the Jaipur that Jai ruled. Gayatri complains that 'subsequent dispensations destroyed the legacy of Jaipur, by design or default because it was not their legacy.'

Jaipur has among other things been the Mecca of Indian polo. In this field, the aura and ambience of Jai's days continues. As an observer noticed, 'Some things still haven't changed at the Jaipur polo scene, the nerve centre of polo in India. Just as a polo match begins, a stray dog enters from the neighbouring golf course, takes offence at the horses, and decides to give them a chase. There are peals of laughter from the spectators and the brave dog abandons its pursuit, lets the horses be, and excuses itself from the field! Likewise, the kites still swoop down on the rolling polo ball mistaking it for a freshly-laid horse egg!'

His state was the focus of Jai's existence. He would return from his trips abroad laden with progressive ideas to be implemented back home. V.P. Menon has stated in his book, *Story of the Integration of Indian States*, that Jaipur became the capital of Rajputana owing to Jai's efforts. In fact, Jai demanded a guarantee on this score before he handed over the state. An ardent lover of architecture, he left behind an awesome range of construction. The Ramgarh Water Works, Maharani Gayatri Devi Girls' School, Sawai Man Singh Hospital, Maharaja's College, Maharani's College, SMS Medical College, Zenana Hospital, Mental Hospital, TB Hospital, Sawai Man Singh Stadium, Rajasthan University, Ram Bagh Golf Course, Secretariat (Bhagwan Das Barracks), Statue Circle (with a statue of Sawai Jai Singh, the founder of Jaipur City), Sanganer Airport, the Man Prakash and Polo Victory theatres, St Xaviers School—all came up during Jai's time.

Jai's departure from the mortal world was followed by the abolition of privy purses. Consequently, the pace and style of the lives of princes changed considerably.

Gayatri maintained her status as a member of parliament by contesting elections to the Lok Sabha against her will and inclination. Despite not involving herself actively in compaigning she won again by more than 50,000 votes.

However, the real bad times were yet to come. During 1975, the income-tax department commenced a search that was to cover Motidoongari, City Palace, Rajmahal, Ram Bagh, Nahargarh, Jaigarh and other places belonging to the erstwhile royal family. The discoveries during the raid were almost comic—nineteen pounds in English money and odd coins of various currencies. Jai had declared all the gold that was found in the earlier searches as personal. The only grudge that the department could have had was the non-payment of tax. It had nothing to do with the legendary Jaipur treasure, which was supposed to have been hoarded in Jaigarh.

The income-tax department was joined by the Foreign Exchange Directorate, the National Geophysical Research Institute of Hyderabad, and the Army Corps of Engineers from Jodhpur. The Jaigarh Fort, a private property, was extensively dug up in search of the elusive treasure.

The police descended on Gayatri's residence at Aurangzeb Road in Delhi on 30 July 1975, with a warrant for her arrest, for contravention of foreign exchange regulations (for possessing nineteen pounds). She was not even allowed to contact her lawyer. Bubbles (Jai's elder son, Bhawani Singh) was present in the house. When he was informed about what was happening, he thought it was a big joke and went out to check. The police arrested him also.

Within five years of Jai's death, his wife and his eldest son were lodged in Tihar Jail under COFEPOSA (Conservation of Foreign Exchange and Prevention of Smuggling Activities). The wife was a sitting member of parliament. The son had just retired from the Army after having won the second highest gallantry award, the Mahavir Chakra, during the 1971 Indo-Pak War.

---

1   It was the *Mah-e-Murtib* that entitled the rulers of Amber the use of the prefix 'Sawai'.

2   Earlier, the heir apparent used to come only till the 'Sireh Deohri' and return to City Palace due to the customary belief that the ruler never dies.

Appendix

THE HISTORY OF THE KACHHWAHAS

The history of Rajputana (Rajasthan) is the history of three Kshatriya Houses: the Kachhwahas of Jaipur (Dhundhar); the Rathores of Jodhpur (Marwar); and the Sisodias of Udaipur (Mewar). The Kachhwahas claim their descent from Kush, the son of Lord Ram, whose life is depicted in the famous epic, the *Ramayana*[1]. The Sisodias of Udaipur claim their descent from Luv, the twin brother of Kush. Both these tribes are Suryavanshis, or descendants of the Sun God, since Lord Ram's lineage is traced back to Surya (the sun). In fact the family priests of the Kachhwahas have contrived to trace their origin back to Brahma, the Creator, one of the gods of the Hindu Trinity, of which Lord Ram was supposed to be the 63rd descendant.

From the kingdom of Ayodhya, which Ram ruled, the Kachhwahas claim to have migrated to Sakit and Rahatas, before establishing themselves around Gwalior and Narwar. Toraman Kachhwaha, the first known Kachhwaha ruler, defeated Devnag of Nagvansh and established his own state with Sihonia (situated near modern Gwalior) as his capital. Toraman's descendant, Maharaja Soor Singh, built the fort of Gwalior supposedly after Gwal Pal, an ascetic whose blessings cured Soor Singh of leprosy. According to the legend, Maharaja Soor Singh lost his way on a hunting excursion and was on the verge of collapse due to thirst and fatigue. Gwal Pal took the king to a spring close by, where the king quenched his thirst. A bath in the spring water, on the advice of the ascetic, cured the maharaja of leprosy. The grateful maharaja widened the spring and erected a fort in its vicinity, which was named after the sage. A tank was built nearby and named Suraj Kund. The sage advised Maharaja Soor Singh to suffix 'Pal' to his name. He prophesied that the dynasty of Maharaja Soor Singh would continue to rule at Gwalior as long as they retained the name 'Pal'. Maharaja Soor Singh, thereafter, renamed himself Suraj Pal.

The Kachhwaha dynasty continued to rule over Gwalior for eight centuries. Maharaja Nala founded Narwar (in Malwa) in A.D. 886. His son Dhola married Maroni, the daughter of Buddh Singh Bhati of Pungal (a kingdom near Jaisalmer). Dhola-Maroni has entered folklore as a couple.

One of the kings, Nand Pal of the Kachhwaha clan, attacked and killed Rajpal, the King of Kanauj, in 1019 for his unpardonable crime of meekly submitting to Mahmood of Gajnavi without a valiant fight. Later, Mahmood vainly tried to avenge this death, but was forced to retreat. This incident is paradoxical in retrospect, because the Kachhwahas of Jaipur have always been accused by the nobility in Rajputana, more particularly by the Sisodias of Mewar, of having submitted to Muslim rule. As we shall see later, these accusations are unfair and ignore the geographic imperatives faced by the rulers of Amber (Jaipur).

Tejkaran aka Dulharai, the last Kachhwaha ruler at Gwalior, moved to Dausa around A.D. 966 on an invitation by his father-in-law, Ralhan Chauhan, who was the king of Lalsot. Badgujars, the sworn enemies of the Chauhans, controlled sizable territory in Dausa. The arrival of Dulharai was to change the pattern and create history.

When Dulharai arrived, the countryside south-east of Amber was being controlled by five family groups of Meenas, a local tribe. However, these five families were not united politically or otherwise, and they largely led isolated existences, holding forts here and there and owing their suzerainty to the Badgujar king. Dulharai was a clever and enterprising warrior who planned his attacks in Napoleonic style. There are many stories of his daring and bravery. He attacked Manchi during a festival (as in the Yom Kippur War[2]) when the Meenas were busy revelling and were easily overpowered. The victory, so says folklore, was due to the blessings of Jamwa Mata, for whom a temple was built on the Ban Ganga River. Jamwa Mata is still considered the family goddess of the Kachhwahas of Amber. Simultaneously, Manchi was renamed Ramgarh to show the Kachahawa claim of descent from Lord Ram. Dulharai, thereafter, attacked and captured the fort of Dehoti belonging to the Badgujars. Kho, Sanganer, and Jhotwara followed. Thus, the area surrounding Amber (which was to be the first capital of the Kachhwahas) was captured. Dulharai's son Kokil, who succeeded his father in A.D. 1070, continued the vigorous expansion by taking Amber from Rao Bhatto. It was Kokil who moved to Amber and laid the foundation of the kingdom. The capital was, however, moved from Manchi to Amber almost six generations later.

Kokil's grandson, Pajvan, was one of the most celebrated heroes of this clan before the Mughal age. He was married to a cousin of Prithvi Raj Chauhan, the ruler of Ajmer and Delhi. Pajvan died fighting rearguard action while Prithvi Raj escaped with Sanyogita.[3] On hearing of his death, Prithvi Raj is supposed to have said, 'Delhi had become a widow, and Dhundhar (Amber) had become masterless.' Pajvan has been immortalized in the famous *Prithvi Raj Raso* by the bard, Chand Bardai.[4] The paeans sung for Pajvan go to show that the Kachhwahas were not stooges of Delhi. Pajvan's descendants, too, wandered far and wide and conquered lands beyond their territories long before Akbar ruled Delhi.

Malesi, the elder son of Pajvan, took over. He had 32 sons and his descendants were as prolific. One of the important lines that was fathered was that of Udaikaran, whose second son Bud Singh founded the Naruka branch (of Alwar, Uniyara, and Lawa). Baloji was a progenitor of the Shekhawat branch. After Pajvan, 10 Kachhwaha generations were engaged in the construction of forts and palaces and temples in the region.

It was around this time that the shrine of Khwaja Moinuddin Chisti, who died in Ajmer in March 1236, was built. Khwaja Makhdum Husain, the chief disciple of Khwaja Chisti, built his mausoleum from donations made by Sultan Ghyasuddin Khilji of Mandu. The construction of this mausoleum at Ajmer cast a long shadow on the events in times to come. It is the second holiest pilgrimage centre for the Muslims, second only to Mecca. Akbar, the first Mughal emperor and the most powerful Mughal king, was an ardent devotee of Khwaja Chisti. He came to visit the shrine on 15 January 1562, after the conquest of Chittor. He walked barefoot from Chittor to Ajmer. The route from the Mughal capital to this shrine led through Amber. It was almost an ordained duty of the Muslim kings to keep the route to Ajmer open. Axiomatically, control of Amber was imperative and had to be attained at all cost. In the situation, Amber was in no position to resist the might of the Mughals.

Some historical documents suggest that Mewar under Maharana Kumbha used to extract tribute from Amber. Prithvi Raj of Amber also took to the field under Rana Sanga of Mewar to fight Babar in what is known as the first battle of Panipat. Prithvi Raj had 12 sons from nine wives. The sons came to be known as Bara Kotdi, or the 12 chambers of the Kachhwaha house, and formed the highest aristocracy of Jaipur. Prithvi Raj's son Pooran Mal ruled for seven short years and died fighting for Humayun in 1543. His son Suja was a child; hence his stepbrother Bhim Singh succeeded him. After Bhim came his eldest son Rattan Singh, who was killed by Askaran on 15 May 1548. Askaran was crowned the next day, but he could rule only for 16 days. His nobles unceremoniously deposed him. Later, he rose high in Akbar's court and was given a vacant Narwar (the Kachhwahas had moved from Narwar to Gwalior). Bihar Mal succeeded Askaran at Amber in 1548.

Bihar Mal's ascension to the throne heralded a new chapter. Those were turbulent times. Delhi's interference in Rajputana affairs, ever present except during the time of Alauddin Khilji two and a half centuries earlier, had increased. Rana Sanga died after Khanua and was succeeded by weak kings in Mewar (ruled by the Sisodias of Udaipur). Amber also passed through similar turbulence and Marwar (the Rathores of Jodhpur) became strong. Maldeo, the Rathore ruler, took four districts from Amber, thus forcing the Kachhwahas to side with the Pathan (that is, Sher Shah Suri) in Delhi. The death of Sher Shah Suri and his son Islam Shah, brought Humayun back to the Delhi throne. Akbar succeeded Humayun and became the king of a shrunken and dissipated empire at the age of 13. The second battle of Panipat in 1556, when Akbar's guardian Bairam Khan defeated Hemu, cleared the way for the pre-eminence of the Mughal Empire.

The child Suja (son of Pooran Mal), sore at being ignored in succession, liased with Mirza Sharfuddin Hussain, Akbar's governor of Mewat. They attacked Amber to seize the throne which, Suja believed, rightfully belonged to him. Unable to face this onslaught, Bihar Mal paid tribute to the Mirza and gave his son Jagannath and two nephews as hostages for due payment. Mirza smelt blood. He planned to annex Amber. Now, Bihar Mal had no option but to seek Akbar's protection. According to Jadunath Sarkar, Bihar Mal used Chagtai Khan as his intercessor to persuade the emperor. Akbar was on his way from Agra to Ajmer. Bihar Mal received him at Sanganer and offered to marry his eldest daughter to Akbar.

The offer and its acceptance rankles the Kachhwahas till date. They are the butt of jokes on Rajput chivalry.

Hindu kings had married their daughters to Muslim rulers even in the past. The Raja of Uchh (Bahawalpur, now in Pakistan) had married his daughter to Shahabuddin Ghori way back in 1176. But, earlier, girls after marriage were as lost to their family as if they would have been if they were kidnapped. Even in Akbar's time, the girl could not visit her parents after marriage. She became a Muslim and was buried in the Muslim cemetery. However, the girl's family achieved status in the king's court. It was the last, a deliberate shift in policy by Akbar, that tempted Bihar Mal. Akbar was keen to forge such alliances with Rajputs since he found his own clan treacherous. Rajputs, whose conduct was based on chivalry and valour, could be trusted.[5]

The marriage took place according to Hindu rites at Sambhar. Bihar Mal presented his eldest son Bhagwant Das and grandson Man Singh, to Akbar. Man Singh's transfer from his grandfather's tutelage to the Mughal court was to have a cascading effect on events for the next 200 years.

Man Singh's rise in the court of Akbar was meteoric. He came to be known more popularly as Raja Man Singh (1589–1614). He was conferred with the title of 'Mirza Raza', Persian words that mean 'born of a king'. The valour and chivalry of Mirza Raja Man Singh was unparalleled. He was considered the brightest jewel among the nine gems of Akbar's court. The exploits and campaigns of Raja Man Singh covered a wide canvas from Afghanistan, Kabul, and Kandhar in the west to Bihar, Orissa, Kamroop,· and Assam in the east, Burhanpur in Maharashtra, and Kashmir in the north.

An incident still recounted by Rajputs occurred when Maharana Pratap, the ruler of Chittor, refused to submit to Akbar's rule. Mirza Raja Man Singh was sent as Akbar's emissary to secure his submission. Maharana Pratap, aware of Raja Man Singh's mission, did not grant him audience. However, as a matter of courtesy, he sent lunch for Raja Man Singh, who felt humiliated and offended. Raja Man Singh took a few grains of rice, put them in the folds of his turban so as not to insult the food, left without eating, and vowed revenge. Subsequently, in the famous battle of Haldi Ghati in 1576, Raja Man Singh triumphed over Maharana Pratap through his sheer brilliance as a general. Though, Maharana Pratap was a brave man, tactics was not his forte. The Sisodias were accomplished in guerrilla tactics, but were uncomfortable fighting a pitched battle. Their discomfort accrued from the fact that they had never really fought battles in the real sense. They would either close the gates of their forts and hold out until the siege lifted, or they would indulge in guerrilla tactics. At Haldi Ghati, a wounded Maharana Pratap had to retreat, and the Mewar army was decimated. There was no pursuit (à la Dunkirk)[6] for which various reasons were ascribed: that Raja Man Singh's troops, fatigued after the hard fight, were in no condition to pursue the defeated enemy; that Raja Man Singh was wary of ambushes by Maharana Pratap's retreating army; and that Raja Man Singh, a noble man, could never have been persuaded to hound a defeated adversary. A fourth theory is that Raja Man Singh permitted a fellow Rajput to retreat without further disgrace or embarrassment. Two incidents support the fourth theory. The first: it was alleged that Mirza Abdul Rahim Khan-e-khanan, son of the well-known Bairam Khan (Akbar's guardian), switched towards Maharana Pratap's side due to Raja Man Singh; the second: when Man Singh was recalled and Shahbaj Khan sent to eliminate the Maharana, Raja Man Singh was alleged to have instigated a Kachhwaha chieftain to kill Shahbaj, which he did, thereby helping Maharana Pratap at Sherpura in 1580.

However, it is worth noting that not pursuing the enemy was a sagacious choice as well. Plundering and looting the fallen foe sows seeds of revolt.[7]

In 1588, Mirza Raja Man Singh was appointed subedar of Bihar and Bengal. He conquered Orissa and was raised to the position of *Mansabdar* of 7,000, the highest distinction ever bestowed upon anyone by the emperor. The title of Mirza was conferred on Raja Man Singh after this feat. Before his death, Akbar called Mirza Raja Man Singh and instructed him to stand by Prince Salim (later Jahangir), who became emperor in 1605. This was indicative of the trust and confidence Raja Man Singh held in Akbar's esteem.

Some historians allege that Raja Man Singh was recalled from Haldi Ghati as Akbar was suspicious of him. The allegation is baseless. Shahbaj Khan was sent to pursue Maharana Pratap so that Raja Man Singh could be used to meet a more imminent danger on the north-west frontier. Akbar relied upon Raja Man Singh to crush enemy advances and quell rebellions. Raja Man Singh was Akbar's troubleshooter when it came to the clearing of the Khyber Pass, or being sent as ambassador to Kabul to suppress the Raushaniyas or convincing the populace of the good intentions of Akbar. Raja Man Singh's career was unsurpassed. The Afghan hills were splattered with the 'best blood' of the Kachhwahas in the campaigns that took place. He was in command of both civil and military affairs. Bihar, in the east, had been an ignored territory till then. It was Raja Man Singh who conquered Bihar, Orissa, and Bengal and reached Assam. His achievements have been immortalized in the *Akbar Nama* in these words: 'The Raja united ability with courage and genius with strenuous action, he administered the province excellently, even the refractory became obedient.'

Raja Man Singh conquered Orissa in 1593. He forayed into east Bengal. Here Laxmi Narain, the king of Cooch Behar (a tiny kingdom), sought Akbar's protection from his cousin Raghu Dev, who was in alliance with Isa Khan. Raja Man Singh went to his rescue and Laxmi Narain gave his sister Kshma Devi in marriage to Mirza Raja Man Singh on 23 December 1596. Another bride from the same place—Gayatri Devi, wife of Sawai Man Singh—was to arrive 400 years later. Raja Man Singh lost two of his brilliant sons Himmat Singh and Jagat Singh in Bengal. On Raja Man Singh's request, he was brought to Amber, but trouble again erupted in Bengal and Man Singh was asked to rush back.

Salim (Jahangir) had proclaimed himself emperor at Allahabad (December 1600). He was addicted to wine, opium, and women. Jahangir's conduct left a lot to be desired, as is evident from the Noor Jahan episode, as well as the murder of Akbar's minister, Abul Fazal, for personal vengeance. Jahangir harboured suspicions about Raja Man Singh, having worked against him during his father's time.

The distrust soon came out in the open. During his third tenure of viceroyalty in Bengal, Raja Man Singh refused to carry out the abominable task of snatching Noor Jahan from her lawful husband, Sher Afghan Istajlu, a minor Turkish *jagirdar* of Burdwan in Bengal and sending her to Jahangir. The task was too delicate for a man of honour and dignity such as Raja Man Singh. However, Jahangir was the emperor and a man possessed. Things were organized without much ceremony. On 20 May 1607, the husband perished, and the maiden was transported to her royal lover.

When Raja Man Singh returned from Bengal to Amber in 1608, he brought with him the idol of goddess Shila Devi, presently located in the temple at Amber Fort.

Raja Man Singh's granddaughter (daughter of his deceased son Jagat Singh) was married to Jahangir. After a visit to Amber for a short while, to recruit more Kachhwahas into the emperor's army, Raja Man Singh was sent to the Deccan merely as one of the three divisional commanders. Prince Parvez was the nominal head of the army. Abdul Rahim Khan-e-khana was the prince's guardian and executive agent. Mismanagement and mutual jealousy led to the humiliating defeat of the imperial forces. Worse, Raja Man Singh passed away a sad man at Ilichpur on 6 July 1614. He left no son suitable for the House of the Kachhwahas. A glorious life had ended in a whimper.

The Kachhwahas are accused of having subjugated themselves before the Mughals. However, history records that Bhagwant Das and Mirza Raja Man Singh were neither timid nor sycophants. They retained their freedom of speech and thought. They refused to embrace Din-e-ilahi, the religion founded by Akbar. They continued to worship Hindu gods and goddesses, whose idols they carried in all their campaigns. The Kachhwahas can truly be called the builders of an empire, under the sovereignty of the Mughals. However, they had to pay an exacting price in their personal lives. They lived far apart from their families for most of their lives and died in places anywhere between the north-west frontier and the Tapti river in the Deccan. From Bhagwant Das who died in December 1589 to Bishan Singh's death in 1699, six successive Kachhwaha kings died away from Amber. Such figures stand in need of no counsel to exhibit the involvement, devotion, and the contribution of the Kachhwahas to this nation.

Historians have not done justice to Mirza Raja Man Singh. He has been accused of wilting before a mighty king. The fact that during Akbar's time he was instrumental in uniting India in the form that we see today, is ignored. Before this, small principalities were nibbling at, wrangling with, and raiding one another constantly. Peace was unknown. While lauding Maharana Pratap and castigating Raja Man Singh, geographical imperatives have been overlooked. Maharana Pratap had the advantage of a hilly terrain (Mewar) best suited to evade the enemy and to resort to guerrilla tactics. Access to Amber from Agra was not only easy and convenient,

but Amber fell on the Agra-Ajmer route. The importance of
Ajmer in those times cannot be overemphasized. The Dargah
of Khwaja Moinuddin Chisti is located here. The mighty
Akbar was a devotee of the Khwaja. Amber, thus, had no
option but to keep peace with Delhi.

The third son of Raja Man Singh, Maharaja Bhao Singh,
was the successor. Jahangir gave him a *Mansab* of 5,000. Bhao
Singh ruled for seven years (1614–1621) and was succeeded
by Mirza Raja Jai Singh (1621–1667). He marked a new
chapter in the history of the Kachhwahas. Mirza Raja Jai
Singh beheld the kaleidoscopic changes that occurred during
the times of Jahangir, Shah Jahan, and the early years of
Aurangzeb. His campaigns covered a vast canvas from
Afganistan (Kandhar) to Monghyr in the east and from
Central Asia (Balkh) to Bijapur and Golconda in the Deccan.
Raja Jai Singh was not only a brilliant general, but also an
excellent diplomat. He knew Persian and Turkish besides
Hindi and Sanskrit. Most of the achievements of Shah Jahan[8]
(when Jai Singh was in his prime) have a strong imprimatur of
Raja Jai Singh. When Jahangir died, Raja Jai Singh was 16 and
had already been a king for five years. During one of his
campaigns, Raja Jai Singh defeated Shahji Bhonsle (father of
the famous Shivaji). Raja Jai Singh's dominance in the
Mughal court continued even during the first decade of
Aurangzeb's rule. However, towards his end, Prince Dara
Shukho became hostile towards Raja Jai Singh. Jaswant
Singh, head of the rival house of Marwar, started getting more
importance.

Mirza Raja Jai Singh played an important role in the battle
of succession, capturing Dara after a hot pursuit and
defeating Sooja.[9] He was made a commander of 7,000, the
highest honour. Raja Jai Singh was a generous man. Having

regained his eminence in the court, he received the title of Maharaja and restored the command of 6,000 to Jaswant Singh on 10 November 1659. Jaswant Singh had lost the title as he deserted troops during the battle of Khajwa.

During this period, the Marathas had become a formidable power. The concerted efforts of the Mughals in taming Shivaji came to naught. Ultimately, in 1664, when he was 65 years of age, Mirza Raja Jai Singh was called upon to lead an army against the redoubtable Shivaji. In the aftermath of their engagement, Shivaji was forced to negotiate peace with Raja Jai Singh at Purander. The agreement reached between him and Shivaji was indicative *inter alia,* of Raja Jai Singh's diplomatic abilities. Despite Shivaji's resistance and reluctance, he was persuaded to attend Aurangzeb's court at Agra. The episode finds a prominent mention in contemporary history.

Shivaji was apparently not happy with the treatment he received in the emperor's court. Raja Jai Singh's son, Ram Singh, tried to pacify Shivaji, but to no avail. Shivaji refused to attend the court again and was, consequently, incarcerated. He escaped through subterfuge. He feigned sickness and ordered a large quantity of fruits to be distributed as alms to poor people to regain his health. When the baskets of fruits were being returned, he hid himself in one of them. The emperor suspected Ram Singh, the son of Raja Jai Singh, of complicity. However, the stature of the Raja Jai Singh, pre-empted any immediate action.

The last ill-fated battle that Mirza Raja Jai Singh fought was at Bijapur. His army was vastly outnumbered. The emperor was not very happy, since the decimated and emaciated Mughal army had to retreat from Bijapur. This was the only military failure of his life. He had spent rupees one

crore of his own money. As Jadunath Sarkar says in *A History
of Jaipur*: 'He died bankrupt after serving too faithfully an
exacting but thankless master.' He died in Burhanpur in 1667,
a disappointed man. He was succeeded by Ram Singh I
(1667–1688) and Bishan Singh (1688–1699), who paled in
comparison to their ancestor. Aurangzeb had Kishan Singh,
the son of Ram Singh and father of Bishan Singh, murdered.
Tragically, this incident does not find mention even in the
footnotes of history.

Jai Singh II (1699–1743), aged 11 years, succeeded Bishan
Singh. He was the founder of Jaipur. In the words of
Jawaharlal Nehru, 'He would have been a remarkable man
anywhere, in any time.' He redeemed the glory of the
Kachhwaha clan and lifted it to a level higher than that of the
great Mirza Raja Man Singh or Mirza Raja Raja Jai Singh. Jai
Singh's life span covers the death of Aurangzeb, the
ransacking of Delhi by Nadir Shah, and the confusion that
followed. He was conferred the title of Sawai (equal to 1 and
1/4).[10] It was during his rule that the forts of Jhilai and Isarda
were included under Kachhwaha jurisdiction. Aurangzeb
always looked on Sawai Jai Singh with suspicion and
malignity. In October 1729, he was appointed the governor of
Malwa. By this time, the Marathas had become very weak.
However, they continued their incursions into the imperial
kingdom. Palace intrigues were rife. The rival nobles were
inciting the emperor against Sawai Jai Singh. In the
meanwhile, Nadir Shah tore Delhi to pieces, ending any
organized government in Delhi. It was under such
circumstances that Sawai Jai Singh fell back to Amber and
planned a local hegemony for Rajputana. He had to contend
with a fracas within Rajputana, involving Bundi, Kota, and
Mewar. Ajit Singh, the Raja of Marwar, was murdered by his

second son, Bakht Singh, in June 1724. Ajit's elder son Abhay Singh then ascended the throne of Marwar and got married to Sawai Jai Singh's daughter.

The Kachhwahas and the Rathores frequently inter-married, but the sons-in-law and fathers-in-law rarely saw eye-to-eye. Abhay Singh's attack on Bikaner was a turning point during this period. Raja Zorawar Singh of Bikaner appealed to Sawai Jai Singh for help. Bikaner lay under siege by the Jodhpur forces of Abhay Singh. Sawai Jai Singh marched with his army directly to Jodhpur, forcing Abhay Singh to lift the siege and compromise, thereby, submitting to the suzerainty of Amber. The nobles of Jodhpur found the humiliation difficult to stomach. Consequently, a battle between Jodhpur and Jaipur followed at Gangwana (near Pushkar). Udaipur brokered peace after bloodshed.

The formal foundation of Jai Nagar, later named Jaipur (City of Victory), was laid in 1727, though the work had started in 1725 itself. Vidhyadhar Chakravrati was the chief architect. 'Founded,' as Nehru said, 'during the darkest period of India's history, when disruption and war and tumult filled the scene, it is symbolic of the spirit of scientific enquiry, which was not dead in India and there was plenty of good material for scientific work in the country, both theoretical and technical, if only it was given a chance to function.'

During Sawai Jai Singh's time, the boundaries of Jaipur State were expanded. The area under Jaipur was larger than that under Delhi. In Akbar's time, Amber was a *pargana* under the *subah* of Ajmer, with revenue earnings of a little over rupees 3 lakh. Fifty-one *parganas* were later wrested from Kaim Khan of Jhunjhunu. Sawai Jai Singh had an army of 30,000 soldiers, and an equal proportion of horsemen and foot musketeers. He was a religious man. He constructed rest houses and free kitchens at Ayodhya, Mathura, and other holy cities. Sawai Jai Singh crowded his short life of 56 years with innumerable achievements. In fact, his active career was longer and more eventful than that of Mirza Raja Jai Singh or even that of the great Mirza Raja Man Singh. He built observatories at Delhi, Jaipur, Ujjain, Mathura, and Benaras. Pedro Emanuel Figuredo was summoned from Italy for this purpose. Sawai Jai Singh's genius in matters scientific and astronomical was nonpareil. He even invented some instruments. Nehru wrote: 'It is not his political or military career that interests me. He was a brave warrior and an accomplished diplomat but he was something much more than this. He was a mathematician and an astronomer, a scientist and a town planner, and he was interested in the study of History.'

Aurangzeb died on 21 February 1707. The seeds his misrule sowed gave fruit: the Mughal Empire was to crumble and crash soon. During the last phase of Aurangzeb's reign, Sawai Jai Singh was a deputy to and favourite of Prince Bidar Bakht. Sawai Jai Singh's half brother Bijay Singh had all along been a refugee in Bahadur Shah's court. Consequently, when Bahadur Shah became the emperor, on his way to Marwar, he stopped at Amber. He made Bijay Singh the king and relegated Sawai Jai Singh to a mere *mansabdar* in January 1708. Amber was renamed Mominabad. However, the emperor had to rush to Deccan. He had by now become too weak to have his fiat imposed. Sawai Jai Singh regained his throne by July 1708. His calibre, which had become clouded towards the end of Aurangzeb's reign and afterwards, got its due recognition in 1713 when he was appointed the viceroy of Malwa.

Sawai Jai Singh's canvas of operations was the largest

among all the Kachhwaha kings. Even politically he was a sagacious person. Seeing Delhi crumbling and the Marathas gaining ascendancy, he safeguarded his kingdom through an alliance with Mewar: he married the Princess of Mewar. This act had far-reaching and unpleasant repercussions. During his mariage he promised to give his throne to his son born of the Princess of Mewar.[11] It was only on this condition that the Maharana had consented to give his daughter in marriage to Jaipur (a family who had given their daughter to the Turks). This slur, right or wrong, became indelible for the Kachhwahas.

Sawai Jai Singh's death on 21 September 1743 at Jaipur, was followed by a 75-year dark period during which Maratha hordes and Pindari freebooters ravaged Jaipur.

Madho Singh I was born of the Mewar Princess in 1738. He had two elder stepbrothers, Shiv Singh and Ishwari Singh. Shiv Singh pre-deceased his father. Ishwari Singh, being the elder, succeeded Sawai Jai Singh in the normal course of events and was recognized by Emperor Mohammed Shah. He was Sawai Jai Singh's favourite son and was crowned the king, despite Sawai Jai Singh's promise to the Maharana of Mewar. However, Ishwari Singh proved himself inadequate as successor. He also did not have a single day of peace in the seven years of his rule, with Bundi, Jodhpur, and the Maharana of Mewar committed to dislodging him. Help was even sought from the Marathas. Ishwari Singh repulsed the first attack in the battle of Rajmahal in 1747 and chased the attacking forces till Bhilwara (Udaipur). Isari Lat was built to celebrate this victory. Later, the Battle of Bagru was fought between the same armies: Jaipur alone and against all the principalities of Rajasthan aided by the marathas. Heavy rains helped Jaipur;

the combine retreated. Soon the Marathas returned. By now they had a mole in Ishwari Singh's durbar, Har Govind Natani, a trusted minister. The poor king realized his folly when Malhar Holkar reached Sanganer. Ishwari Singh had been kept in the dark about the enemy's location, strength, and even the strength of Jaipur's forces. He was told the truth once Holkar was upon Jaipur. Ishwari Singh had no option left. He got himself bitten by a cobra and consumed poison. His four queens and one concubine followed suit.

His half-brother Madho Singh I (1750–1768) from the Mewar princess took over. He founded the city of Sawai Madhopur. When the Marathas tried to enter Jaipur again in 1753, Madho Singh I made peace by offering tribute. Thereafter, Jaipur was free from the Maratha menace for about three years.

Bharatpur was a nobility of Jaipur under a Jat chieftain. Jawahir Singh of Bharatpur began indulging in activities inimical to Jaipur State. The Jat Raja took Narnol district with the help of the Sikhs. Later, Madho Singh I thrashed Jawahir Singh at Maonda in 1767. The military glory of Jaipur recovered a little during Madho Singh I's time.

After Madho Singh I there were a succession of minor rulers (from 1768 to 1839) with the queen mothers calling the shots. The Kachhwaha nobles did not like this. The splendid heritage of Mirza Raja Man Singh and Mirza Raja Jai Singh sat cheek by jowl with the Turks' outposts just 12 kms off Jaipur city. Jaipur lost 48 *parganas*; only four remained. In those days the extraction of tribute by coercion was common. Jaipur was surrounded by hounds looking for their pound of flesh. Somehow or the other, the Kachhwahas always protracted the negotiations on the terms of the tribute, often succeeding in starving the aggressor party.

The 10-year reign of Prithvi Singh (1768–1778), who succeeded Madho Singh I, is marked by the first contact of the Kachhwahas with the British in 1776. However, the contact was of no avail. Pratap Singh succeeded him. The reign of Sawai Pratap Singh (1778–1803) is another sad chapter in Kachhwaha history, primarily because he chose wrong advisors. Weak regents were ruling Delhi in short bursts. The Marathas were getting stronger under Mahadji Scindia (the Scindias subsequently ruled Gwalior) and were exercising paramount power. The Jaipur court was also required to pay a large tribute, but Jaipur found it difficult to keep to its promises. Col. James Tod wrote about Pratap Singh: 'A gallant prince, not deficient in judgment but neither gallantry not prudence could successfully apply the resources of his state against the numerous predatory forces and internal dissension.' To an extent, they succeeded in taking advantage of the internal quarrels and weak governments in Delhi. Mahadji first invaded Jaipur in 1786 to exact the tribute, which was settled at Rs 63 lakh. The burden was awesome. Eleven lakhs were paid to ward off the immediate threat, and an alliance was formed with Jodhpur to pre-empt aggressive forays. Efforts were made to rope in English mercenaries. However, Mahadji was back again. Pratap Singh withdrew to his fort, shut himself up, and prepared to stand up to the siege. Mahadji himself led the advance. There were massive desertions. Bikaner and Bundi came to the aid of Jaipur. Mahadji lost his two-and-a-half-year-old daughter, whom he dearly loved, while camping on the outskirts of Jaipur. Simultaneously, he received a challenge to a battle from the Jaipur Raja.

The battle took place at Tunga in 1787, where both sides suffered heavy causalities and each claimed itself victor.

Mahadji was ultimately starved out of Rajputana. While retreating, he is alleged to have said, 'If I live, I shall reduce Jaipur and Jodhpur to dust.' The Rajputs should have expected the vengeance and ought to have prepared themselves accordingly. However, no prophylactic action was taken, and history had to repeat itself.

Pratap Singh had ascended the throne at the age of 13 in 1778. The Hawa Mahal (Palace of Wind) was built during this time. He was a poet as well as a warrior, but found himself helpless. Mahadji revisited Jaipur in 1790. The Kachhwahas had lost these three years in vainly trying to establish their authority over refractory vassals and recovering the territories that were whittling away. No fighting force had been pieced together. Thus, no early action could be taken to counter the Maratha menace. The Kachhwahas were soundly defeated, this time at Patan. Gallant and wholehearted support from Jodhpur was of no avail. Mahadji had come with the redoubtable French general, de Boigne. Peace was negotiated with a payment of Rs 17 lakh. A separate tribute was paid to Holkar. Even though Mahadji died in June 1794, the Marathas continued to trouble the Kachhwahas. The burden of the tribute was getting more crushing and galling by the day. Another battle between the Marathas and the Kachhwahas was fought in 1800 at Malpura. The war between Scindia and Holkar in Poona gave respite to Pratap Singh. He died in 1803 and was succeeded by Jagat Singh (1803–1819).

Sawai Jagat Singh had died childless. One Mohan Singh of Narwar (whence Kachhwahas came) with the complicity of some *jagirdars* was renamed Man Singh and enthroned. The adventure failed when it was learnt that one of the queens of Jagat Singh was pregnant. Jai Singh III was a posthumous child born to this queen. A counsel of regency under the queen mother, with Rawal Bairi Sal (of Samod) as the chief minister, was established. Jhuta Ram Saraogi, a courtier, and Rupa Badaran, a maid, had become powerful during this time. They were the trusted lieutenants of the queen mother. The duo became all powerful and practically frustrated all the efforts of Rawal Bairi Sal of Samod to improve the state of affairs in Jaipur. Bairi Sal banished Jhuta Ram from Jaipur for some time, but he managed to return soon. The queen mother died in 1834 and the minor king, Jai Singh III, died a year later in 1835, under suspicious circumstances.

On Basant Panchami day in 1835, when the young Maharaja Jai Singh's procession was being taken out, the maharaja said something to Rao Jivan Singh of Duni. Jhuta Ram noticed this and thought that there was a scheme to oust him. In the evening he took Jai Singh III to an isolated room and assassinated him. The body was rolled in a tent and placed in a corner. The maharaja was not heard of for the next two days. It was then announced that he had died of a urinary problem. Riots broke out, and Jai Singh III had to be cremated under a cordon of sepoys around the body. The restless crowd pelted Jhuta Ram's group with stones. Simultaneously, a rumour spread that the king had been murdered to ensure British annexation of the state. Public fury became uncontrollable. An assistant political agent, Mr Black, was lynched on his way back from City Palace. After a judicial enquiry, two people were hanged. Jhuta Ram Saraogi and another were incarcerated. Jhuta Ram died later in prison.

While the British had been approached as early as in 1776 by Sawai Prithvi Singh (1768–1778), a temporary treaty of alliance came to be signed with Marquess Wellesley in 1803.

His successor Lord Cornwallis, repudiated the treaty. The volte face was in the face of the fact that a British army unit had been raised by the Kachhwaha king's aid and that ample supplies had also been provided. Even Kachhwaha troops had joined them. An Englishman reflected on this repudiation in the following words: 'This was the first time, since the English Government was established in India, that it had been known to make its faith subservient to its convenience.' However, another treaty was later signed in 1818, with the Marquess of Hastings. During the intervening years, Scindia, Holkar, Amir Khan, and the Pindaries, mercilessly plundered the states of Jaipur, Udaipur, and Jodhpur. Considering the impoverished state of the Jaipur treasury, the terms of the treaty with the British required no payment for the first year. Four, five, six, seven and eight lakhs were to be paid for the succeeding five years and, thereafter, eight lakhs in perpetuity. The Kachhwahas had been devoted generals of the Mughals, and Jaipur always enjoyed Mughal patronage and protection. A weak Delhi had left Jaipur vulnerable to rapacious raiders from the south. The treaty with the British was to herald a period of comparative peace.

The period from 1768 (death of Madho Singh I) to the establishment of the British-controlled counsel in 1839, when Ram Singh II was four years old, can be called the darkest period in the history of the Kachhwahas. Minors occupied the throne for 46 years. In addition, even when the princes came of age, they were hardly mature or qualified to tackle the magnitude of the problems plaguing the state. Nor could they command the unswerving loyalty of the local chieftains. Sawai Jagat Singh's rule (1803–1819) was the nadir. It came after the repudiation of the treaty with the British and before the second (and permanent) one could be signed not only did the severing of the alliance provide a licence to Holkar, but also to his Pathan ally Amir Khan, sparking internal revolts. Jagat Singh was intoxicated by the charm of a danseuse, Raskapoor. His father, Pratap Singh, had been smitten by Didar Baksh. Jagat Singh wanted the courtiers to respect Raskapoor as a queen. This brew resentment, which later snowballed into a disaster. Raskapoor was finally incarcerated in Nahargarh and spent the rest of her days in solitude.

This period is also marked by the most shameful and tragic death of the beautiful Princess Krishna Kumari of Udaipur in 1810. She was betrothed to Maharaja Bheem Singh of Jodhpur who died in 1803 before the knot could be tied. She was then betrothed to Jagat Singh of Jaipur, but Bheem Singh's son, Man Singh, the next king of Jodhpur, claimed her as his bride. The Kachhwahas intervened. Jodhpur intercepted the gifts of betrothal being transported from Udaipur to Jaipur. Jaipur Forces marched to Jodhpur and laid siege to the Mehrangarh fort. Singh in *House of Marwar* writes: 'The wily Amir Khan went to Udaipur and got the princess poisoned by her own aunt, with the knowledge of her father. No bigger blot can ever be cast on the three famous kingdoms of Rajputana.'

Sawai Ram Singh II, the next raja, was 16 months old when Jai Singh III died in 1835. This was a turning point in the history of Jaipur. He was trained under the guidance of a British political agent. Sawai Ram Singh's tenure (1835–1880) can be divided roughly into two parts, 1857 being the watershed. Sawai Ram Singh took to alcohol as soon as he was invested with full powers. There is an unconfirmed story that he used to be drunk from morning till evening. Once, he was in an inebriated state as usual, when the British resident called. Immediately, on the departure of the resident,

Sawai Ram Singh's servant threw his decanter down and left. The servant was summoned the next day to explain his arrogant behaviour. The servant replied that he was embarrassed and ashamed to see his master in such a state, more so in front of the resident. It is said that a repentant Sawai Ram Singh gave a *jagir* of one village to the servant and never touched liquor again.

During the Revolt of 1857, Sawai Ram Singh II asserted himself in favour of the English and won their confidence. In fact all the three heads of the highest clans of the Kshatriyas, the Sisodias (Maharana Saroop Singh), Rathores (Maharaja Takht Singh), and Kachhwahas (Sawai Ram Singh II) supported the English. Although their help may not have been substantial in terms of men and material, the moral effect on the Hindu psyche was disproportionately high, since all other provinces took a cue from them. A grateful British government showered titles on Ram Singh II.

It was during Sawai Ram Singh's tenure that a depleted treasury improved. The state's debt to bankers was cleared and the arrears to the East India Company were also cleared, in no less measure, courtesy the discovery of the hidden treasure of Jhuta Ram Saraogi in 1844. The treasure was revealed by Rupa Badaran, a female courtier and an accomplice of Jhuta Ram, to save her skin. Until now, the state revenues had been prodigiously wasted. Baseless stories abound regarding treasures brought during the time of Mirza Raja Man Singh and later the two Jai Singhs. The fact is that Sawai Ram Singh II inherited a state with empty coffers and a crushing debt. In the post-Aurangzeb period, the Marathas and Pindaries, who engaged mercenaries from France and Portugal, ravished Jaipur. Jodhpur and Udaipur were indifferent spectators to the molestation. Ironically, the thakurs of Jaipur contributed to the decay by refusing to pay their dues. However, financial as well as social reforms were initiated during Sawai Ram Singh's period. The practice of *sati* was abolished and so was bonded labour; dowry was also banned. Although Sawai Jai Singh had also tried to ban the dowry system and infanticide, he had not succeeded.

Sawai Ram Singh II had started attending the meetings of the regency council since the age of 16. Consequently, he gained immense experience. His genius was reflected in the subsequent improvement of Jaipur on all fronts, including administration. Separate departments for police, health, education, survey, and settlement were established. The kingdom was divided into five districts. A royal council was formed. Portfolios were distributed and the town hall was built. Civil and criminal courts were established. Great emphasis was laid on education. A school of art and a medical school were started. Sawai Ram Singh II played a lead role in the establishment of the Mayo College at Ajmer. Metal-top roads and drains were built. Regular municipal committees were nominated. Streets were lit initially by kerosene lamps and, later, by petromax. Jaipur was connected to Agra, Ajmer, and Delhi, by rail. The public library came up in 1871 and the Ram Prakash theatre came up in 1879. There was a great famine in 1868–1869 and the maharaja worked to ameliorate the condition of his subjects.

Sawai Ram Singh II was a great devotee of Shiva, the 'destroyer' god of the Hindu Trinity.[12] He also had the reputation of being one of the most enlightened kings. He wanted to make Jaipur a second Calcutta. Jaipur was founded by Sawai Jai Singh II, but was embellished and adorned by Sawai Ram Singh II. The Ram Niwas garden, the museum, Albert Hall and Ram Bagh Palace were all built during his time. State revenues rose from less than Rs 30 lakh to Rs 61 lakh. When Sawai Ram Singh II had taken over, internal security was practically non-existent. Local chieftains plundered at will. Sawai Ram Singh II tightened the administration and became deeply involved with public welfare. There are many stories of his nocturnal wanderings. The king would wear a disguise so that he could see first hand the plight of the common man. He started the Jaipur Water Works (1875), the Gas Works (1878), The Maharaja's College (1844), The Sanskrit College (1865), The Noble School (1862), The Girls' School (1867), and the Public Works Department (1860). Sawai Ram Singh II was fond of flying kites and the tradition continues to this day. Billiards, polo, cricket, photography, ballroom dances, and topographic surveys were some things he inaugurated. He was also the one to give Jaipur its pink face. He was undoubtedly one of the ablest kings of the Kachhwaha clan.

Sawai Ram Singh II died childless on 17 September 1880. What persuaded him to adopt Kayam Singh of Isarda (later Madho Singh II), a 19-year-old sepoy in the Tonk infantry will always remain a mystery—more particularly since his consent for adoption had been taken on his deathbed.

However, with this, the direct line of the Kachhwahas who had ruled for centuries over far-flung places, ended.

---

1   According to Hindu mythology, Lord Ram was the husband of Sita. Ravana, the king of Ceylon (now Sri Lanka), abducted Sita during her husband's exile from Ayodhya. Rama killed Ravana to rescue Sita, an event remembered every year during Dussera. The victorious return of Ram to Ayodhya is also celebrated as the festival of lights (Deepawali).

2   Egypt and Syria launched an attack on Yom Kippur day in 1973, catching Israel off guard and retrieving most of the territories lost in the wars of 1947-1949,

1956 and specially in the Six Day War of 1967. How the war ended is a different story though.

3   Jai Chand had organized his daughter Sanyogita's *Swayamwar*, a ceremony in which the bride selects her groom by garlanding the chosen one from among the many eligible men invited. Prithvi Raj Chauhan was not invited. To add insult, his statue was kept at the doorkeeper's place. It is rumoured that Sanyogita ignored the invitees and garlanded the statue. Prithvi Raj who was hiding nearby galloped away with her—with Jai Chand's forces on his heels.

4   Chand Bardai wrote: 'As the wind sweeps through a garden uprooting trees, so did Pajvan move killing Mirs and forming heaps of the slain. Pajvan moved about in the army of Muslims like an intoxicated elephant uprooting and scattering with ease, a dense tangle of lotus leaves.'

5   Udai Singh of Jodhpur married his daughter, Mani Bai, to Prince Salim, Akbar's son and the future Jahangir. Shah Jahan, who built Taj Mahal, was her son. Singh in *The House of Marwar* records that earlier Jooha and Maldev had also given Rathore princesses to Muslims, but these earlier alliances were on equal terms. Again in 1715, Maharaja Ajit Singh's daughter was married to Farukh Siyar.

6   German forces under Guderian surrounded Dunkirk after the *blitzkrieg* in 1939. Hitler ordered them not to enter the city. This inexplicable directive baffles military historians till date. This permitted the British Army and the entire British Navy to make good their escape, safely.

7   The Nazis were to learn this lesson much later in 1942, in the Russian campaign. Here, Shabhaj Khan, Akbar's trusted lieutenant, pursued Maharana Pratap in a subsequent campaign, killing peasants en route and thus antagonizing the populace. Thanks to such reckless misadventure, immediately on Shabhaj's return, Maharana Pratap practically regained his kingdom.

8   Shah Jahan had the Taj Mahal constructed at Agra in the memory of his wife. His flair for extravagant architecture necessitated increasing taxes, which distressed his subjects. His son, Aurangzeb, imprisoned him to become the king in 1658.

9   Dara and Sooja were the sons of Shah Jahan.

10   It is believed that in those days the emperor used to retain the conquered territory but the spoils used to be divided equally among the kings leading the attack. Raja Jai Singh's valour and achievements surpassed all contemporaries. Hence he used to get a quarter more than others. Thus, the title 'Sawai', that is, 1 and 1/4.

11 The Udaipur princess was to be treated as his senior wife. He was to sleep with her on all the festival nights, rest in her palace on returning from a battle, and her palanquin was to be the foremost in a procession.

12 During his time, a controversy related to putting *tilak* on the forehead of the priest and the idols erupted. The followers of Vishnu and Shiva mark the *tilak* differently. Devotees of Vishnu have vertical lines in the shape of a 'U' and Shiva's followers make horizontal lines. It is alleged that one Bakshi Ram Vyas misguided Sawai Ram Singh over the matter. The followers of Vishnu left Jaipur and returned only after his death. The episode is famous in the history of Jaipur as *'Tilakon Ka Jhagara.'*

BIBLIOGRAPHY

Collins, Larry and Dominique Lapierre, *Freedom at Midnight*, Collins, London, 1975.

Crewe, Quentin, *The Last Maharaja: A Biography of Sawai Man Singh II*, Michael Joseph Ltd., London, 1985.

Devi, Gayatri and Santha Rama Rau, *A Princess Remembers– The Memoirs of the Maharani of Jaipur*, Weidenfeld & Nicolson, London, 1976.

Galbraith, J.K., *Ambassador's Journal: A Personal Account of the Kennedy years*, Hamish Hamilton, London, 1969.

Ismail, Sir Mirza, *My Public Life*, George Allen & Unwin, London, 1954.

Lal, Keshar, Ajmera Jain & Jawahar Lal Jain (eds.), *Jaipur Album*, The Rajasthan Directories Publishing House, Jaipur.

Menon, V.P., *The Story of the Integration of the Indian States*, Orient Longman, Hyderabad, 1956.

Nehru, Jawaharlal, *The Discovery of India*, Meridian Books, London, 1960.

Robin, Barnett R., *Feudal Revolt and State-Building–The 1938 Sikar Agitation in Jaipur*. South Asian Publishers, New Delhi, 1983.

Rudolph, Susanne Hoeber, Llyod I. Rudolph with Mohan Singh kanota, *Reversing the Gaze: Amar Singh's Diary, A Colonial Subject's Narrative of Imperial India*, Boulder, Co.: Westview, 2002.

Sarkar, Jadunath, *History of Jaipur—c. 1503-1939*, revised and edited by Raghubir Singh, Orient Longman Ltd., New Delhi, 1984.

Singh, Kesari, *Hints on Tiger Shooting*, The Hindustan Times Ltd., New Delhi, 1965.

Shastri, Heera Lal, *Pratyaksh Jeevan Shashtr*, Ajmera Printing Works, Jaipur.

Singh, Dhananajaya, *The House of Marwar: The Story of Jodhpur*, Roli Books, New Delhi, 1996.

Singh, Karni, *The Relations of the House of Bikaner with the Central Powers, 1465-1949*, Manohar Publications, New Delhi, 1974.

Tod, J., *Annals and Antiquities of Rajasthan, or the Central and Western States of India,* Routledge & Kegan Paul, London, 1950.